OLD
OAKVILLE

David Peacock

Suzanne Peacock

OLD OAKVILLE

A character study
of the town's early buildings
and of the men who built them

DAVID & SUZANNE PEACOCK

HOUNSLOW

ISBN 0-88882-040-2

Hounslow Press
A member of the
Dundurn Group

Publisher: Anthony Hawke
Photographer: Patrick Knox
Editor: John Robert Colombo
Designer: David Peacock
Printer: Metrolitho Inc.

Publication was assisted by the **Canada Council**, the **Book Publishing Industry Development Program** of the **Department of Canadian Heritage**, the **Ontario Arts Council**, and the **Ontario Publishing Centre** of the **Ministry of Culture, Tourism and Recreation**.

Second Printing: May 1995
Printed and bound in Canada

To
Gregory
and
Gabrielle

Hounslow Press
2181 Queen Street East
Suite 301
Toronto, Ontario, Canada
M4E 1E5

Hounslow Press
73 Lime Walk
Headington, Oxford
England
OX3 7AD

Hounslow Press
1823 Maryland Avenue
P.O. Box 1000
Niagara Falls, NY
U.S.A. 14302-1000

CONTENTS

PREFACE

This book does not pretend to be an architectural text. Nor is it intended to be a history book. This book is a character study of the old buildings of Oakville, the men who built them and the families that lived in them. It is an invitation to stroll the shaded streets, past the house of the ship's captain, past the mariner's cottage, past the labour of love that was the carpenter's home. It is an invitation to imagine the carriages drawing up to the bells of St. Andrew's; to hear the wagons complain as they crawl up the hill from the harbour; to catch a glimpse of Weller's coach as it pauses at the hotel to let the travellers take refreshment; or to listen for the sounds of the picnickers as they swarm down the gangplank of the excursion boats on a Sunday afternoon.

This book hopes to trace the evolution of social history in the town by studying the architectural styles of nineteenth-century Oakville and how they were influenced by environment, by fashion, by social status, and by the people who were the inhabitants. The purpose is to take a look at these architectural influences so that they might serve as reminders of our good fortune. Old Oakville is still alive!

The sources of reference for this text include Registry Office documents, Assessment Rolls, Tax Collector's Rolls, Church records, cemetery records, newspapers, directories, interviews, and inspections. As a starting point the authors acknowledge the late Mrs. Hazel Mathews' book *Oakville and the Sixteen*

as an invaluable source of information. If the authors of *Old Oakville* have differed on some points with what has been stated in Mrs. Mathews' book, it is only because after twenty-five years new evidence has been uncovered and old facts have been buried by time. The authors have attempted to minimize speculation and made every effort to substantiate information with multiple verification, yet it is inevitable that the authors may have come to some conclusions that will in the future, in the light of new information, prove to be incorrect. The following disclaimer from the preface of the *County of Halton Gazetteer and Directory* of 1869-70 most aptly states the feelings of the authors of *Old Oakville.*

"The first edition of the County of Halton Gazetteer and Directory is here presented to the public, with that degree of diffidence which a profound anxiety with regard to its thoroughness, accuracy and general usefulness would naturally occasion in the mind of its author, and yet with the consciousness that every effort has been made to ensure its fullest efficiency. It is believed that the book will be found as accurate as works of this character usually are, and taking into consideration the many sources from which the information had to be obtained, the compiler would ask the kind indulgence of its many patrons and the public to overlook any omissions or errors that may be found in its pages."

Oakville, Ontario
February, 1979

ACKNOWLEDGEMENTS

The authors would like to thank the many people who opened their homes, their family albums, and their memories, for without their help this book could not have been written. We were overwhelmed by the generous offerings of time and information by all concerned, and would like to give particular thanks to Mr. C. Daniel Chisholm and Lieutenant Colonel Ralph G. Young. It is not possible to name each person who contributed to our research, but the authors wish to acknowledge the assistance of Christine Castle, Curator of the Oakville Museum; Wayne Vickery, Bud Brown, and the Parks and Recreation staff of the Town of Oakville; the staff of the Halton County Registry Office in Milton; The Reverend Canon Ian M. Dingwall, Rector of St. Jude's Church, Reverend K. James Campbell of St. John's United Church, and The Reverend Helen L. Goggin of Knox Presbyterian Church for the use of church records; the archivists at the Archives of Ontario in Toronto; Mrs. Pam Manson-Smith at the School of Architecture Library, University of Toronto; and the staff of the Metropolitan Toronto Library. We are indebted to the late Hazel C. Mathews for her book *Oakville and the Sixteen* and related papers; the late Colonel Walter Moorhouse for his early research and photographs; Mr. Ernest Wilson for his publication *A History of St. John's United Church 1832-1972*; and the Oakville Historical Society for its support of our project.

The authors wish to thank Dover Publications Inc. of New York for permission to quote the 1969 reprint of A. J. Downing's *The Architecture of Country Houses*, first published in 1850.

We would like to congratulate Patrick Knox on his fine photographic studies and Victor Mayes on his darkroom skills. The authors are indebted to the Oakville Museum for the use of photographs in its archives; the Province of Ontario Archives for the use of maps; Mr. and Mrs. Charles Sale for the MacDougald House floor plans and early photograph; Mr. Walter Adamson for the photograph of Potter's Folly; Lieutenant Colonel and Mrs. Ralph G. Young for the opportunity to reproduce the Elizabeth Wilkes watercolour; Mrs. Rhea Banfield for the loan of photographs taken by the late Arnold Banfield; Mr. and Mrs. Syd A. Vince for the use of early photographs of the C. P. Chisholm House; Miss Thelma Meyers for the use of *Town of Oakville Bylaws* and Joan Doty Turnbull for the George Sumner diaries which proved to be an invaluable source of information. Finally we would like to thank John White and Tony Hawke for their vision, their encouragement, their patience, and their faith in our abilities.

BACKGROUND

By 1805 all the lands bordering the north shore of Lake Ontario had been divided into townships except for the tract of bush between Burlington Bay and the Etobicoke River. That tract was the Reserve of the Missisauga Indians, and it was only with the Missisauga Purchase in that year, wherein the Indians surrendered the majority of their fishing and hunting rights, that the British Government opened up the area for settlement. The Dundas Street, now Highway No. 5, surveyed earlier as a military road served as the basis for a grid to lay out the lines and concessions and the last three townships, including the new Trafalgar Township.

The land, covered with a virgin forest of hardwoods and towering pines, some as much as two hundred feet in height, was a dark and foreboding place. This wilderness did not, however, prevent the courageous invasion of a few hardy pioneering families. Their survival depended on the speed with which they could cut and burn the trees so that the sun could shine through on the first crop. The Post family carved out a home on the 7th Line at the Dundas Street. The McCraney family built west of what was to become the townsite of Oakville. Barnett Griggs built east of the townsite, and a few years later increased the size of his home to accommodate travellers and established the Halfway House. A mile further east, Joshua Leach set up a sawmill beside his new homestead. All were courageous folk who set out to conquer this wild land.

It was the mouth of the Sixteen Mile Creek and the flat lands bordering it that attracted the attention of William Chisholm. It was one of the last reserves of the Missisauga Indians who still hunted, fished, and farmed there. Chisholm realized the great potential of the river mouth as a harbour and the access it provided to the rich country in the north.

Born in Shelburne, Nova Scotia, in 1788, of Scottish descent, Chisholm moved with his Loyalist family to a farm on Burlington Bay in 1794. After fighting in the war of 1812, Chisholm began farming in Nelson Township. Shortly thereafter this enterprising young man opened a general store and began buying wheat, timber, and oak barrel staves from the area. As a merchant he was both importer and exporter for the district and within a few years he amassed considerable wealth. Chisholm furthered his forwarding business by building his own fleet of schooners to carry his goods up and down the lake.

As his financial interests grew, so did his participation in governmental affairs. In 1820, he became a member of the House of Assembly and served as a commissioner to supervise the construction of the Burlington Bay Canal and later the Welland Canal. In 1824, with his connections in high places and a sizeable bank account, he began his pursuit of the land at the mouth of the Sixteen. After considerable lobbying, William Chisholm purchased by public auction from the Crown in August of 1827 the 960 acres that were to become the Town of Oakville. He paid the sum of £1,029 or $4,116. The Missisauga Indians were relocated and the monies from the sale of their lands were used to establish for them a village of log houses on what is now the site of the Mississauga Golf Club.

The shallow waters at the mouth of the Sixteen allowed construction of piers to begin almost immediately, and a community of shanties, lean-to's, and log cabins quickly appeared. A grist and saw mill were started. That first winter of 1827-28, a hotel was erected under the charge of William Young who served as its proprietor until his death in 1831. The new proprietor, William Sumner, was a seasoned tavernkeeper who added a

second storey when he took over the lease from Chisholm. The Oakville House grew as the town and the needs of the inhabitants grew.

Later the structure was enlarged by a third storey and still later by a three-storey addition to the east. Consequently, what began as a simple, one-storey structure with five openings grew to ten, to fifteen, and then to twenty-one bays. The Oakville House, through black days and dry periods, continued to operate as a hotel and is believed to be the oldest continuously operated hotel in Ontario. Although it has been greatly altered over the years, the basic structure still stands to serve as a physical cornerstone of old Oakville and as a symbol of the potential inherent in many of the existing old buildings.

POSTSVILLE

MUNN'S CORNERS

D U N D A S   S T R E E T

Wm. Clark

Edgar Carpenter

Arthur Bentley

Geo Taylor

Henry William

John Airey

Geo Lampeer

Geo Taylor

Edwd Cornwell

Mrs. Eliza Wilson

Edwd Cornwell

Saml Shain

Chas. Culham

Henry Albertson

Kelley

Hugh Mulholland

Mrs. Mary Hardy

Josh Clark

Geo. Tindill (Blacksmith)

Wm. Kaitting

Wm.Y. Pettit

Mrs. J. Bigger

Geo. Mulholland

Saml Kenney

K. H. Munn

Paul P. Crosby

Hiram Post

Jas. Williamson

John Gilby

Chas. Freeman

Levi Lewis

Solo. Savage

Chas Culham

John Culham

Chas Culham

John Culham

Mrs M. Leach

J.B.Anderson

J.L. Bigger

John Gray

Robt Freeman

Robt Hanham

Chas. McDuffie

Wm. Coot Hill View

Chas. Coot Hill View

Mrs. S. Albertson

R. Scott

M.C.

D.

D.S.

Rodk McNeil

Edmond W. Odell

Hiram McCraney Mount Farm

W. M. King

Hiram McCraney

John Aiton

Jas. Robertson

John Foreman

J.R. Anderson

Robt McNeil

Rich. Coates Thornton Farm

Barnet Griggs

Saml Harris

Benjn Griggs

John Rutlege

Jas. Carter

Benjn Thomas

John McKay

S.M.

Robt K. Chisholm

DEPÔT

S. Williams

J. Parsons

R. Humphill

W. Moon

Onice Murphy

Saml Williams

Edn Quarrie

W. Willoughby

Rich. of Hopgood

Geo Griggs

R. McNeil

John Carter

Dav. Lebar

Hiram McCraney

J. Terry

Mrs. F. A. Greeniss

J. Leach Heir

R. Hopgood

R. Coates

Josh Kenney

Geo Washington Parsonage

Andw Lebar

M. Thomas

John Thomas

George K. Chisholm Esq.

TOWN OF OAKVILLE

J. Beardsley

J. J.

B. Griggs

Wm Cantrey Dunburn Cottage

Lighthouse

INTRODUCTION

With William Chisholm's final payment to the Crown in March of 1831, the townsite was surveyed and laid out in a grid system of streets and building lots. The first public sale of lots took place in May of 1833, and in July of 1834 a declaration was published, announcing another upcoming auction of fifty of the most valuable "Town lots" and "Water lots." The terms were one-half the purchase price, payable at the time of sale, the other half to be paid within twelve months. The announcement further stated the condition that a structure, no less than twenty-four feet by eighteen feet, be erected on the lot within eighteen months of the day of sale, and that this structure be of stone, brick, or frame construction.

After the original settlers survived the first few winters, and could afford to do so, their log cabins and shanties were relegated to out-buildings and animal shelters, as it was the desire of every man to live in a fine house with sleeping rooms and plaster walls. The explicit terms of the sale, restricting the materials and governing the size of the buildings, served to ensure the orderly appearance of the growing village.

In the nineteenth century, just as today, the purchase of a home was the greatest single acquisition a man could make. A man's home was a reflection of his character to all who passed by. His home displayed his level on the social register of life, for it was generally accepted that if you lived in a fine house you must be a fine gentleman indeed. It was often thought the origin of the occupant could be determined by the type of house he lived in. To generalize, a Loyalist from the American colonies built an impressive two-storey frame dwelling. It usually boasted delicate ornamentation. It was painted white with green painted shutters. Whereas an English colonist built a modest, plain, one-storey house of brick or frame with a stucco finish.

It was not really as simple as that. Of the people who first settled Oakville, some were native-born in Upper Canada, many more were of Loyalist background, and others (and by far the largest group as the town grew) were English, Scottish, and Irish immigrants. Add to this mixture a number of French Canadians from Lower Canada and a group of Negroes from the United States, and one will begin to see why Oakville is not a homogeneous Williamsburg but rather a *pot-pourri* of individual tastes, reflecting a variety of origins and architectural styles.

There were no houses in Oakville, or in all Ontario, to rank with the finest representatives of colonial architecture in the United States. Very few dwellings were designed by architects in Canada. Few were erected by master builders, and few carpenters or masons worked with pattern books. Only rarely were such treasured handbooks as the *Architectural Assistant*, *The American Builder's Companion*, or the *Builder's Jewel* in the rough and calloused hands of the early builders of Oakville. A house expressed the personality of the owner, not the carpenter, but very few owners were capable of detailing plans for a house. Consequently owners and carpenters working together were the joint architects of this town.

One architect who did practise in Oakville inserted the following advertisement in the *Semi-Weekly Sentinel* on December 2, 1855: "Thomas Coughlan, For many years connected with architecture in most of the cities of Canada and the United States, having removed to Oakville is prepared to furnish plans and specifications to parties intending to build and flatters himself that as he has applied himself to the theory and practice of Building for twenty years that he can give satisfaction."

The early settlers of Oakville were full of adventure, optimism, and new ideas and this compensated for their lack of formal training. The craftsman followed the rules he had learned in his youth in the apprentice system. He was usually a capable, skilled workman who worked instinctively, but the responsibility for design was dictated by the taste of his client, the owner.

The basic design may have stemmed from the fading memories of a Georgian townhouse, been tempered by the then-current Neo-Classic style, and accented with the bravado of a Regency or Revival touch. Few early buildings in Oakville are pure in any one architectural mode. They are vernacular in nature with borrowed forms from past and present. The designs of the structures were determined by environment, financial means, social fashions, and personal whims. They relate the history of the town, not in a political sense, but rather as an evolution of a way of life.

In the beginning, necessity was the dictator of most decisions. The size of the cellar was whatever the owner deemed necessary. It varied from a pit in the earth, accessible by a trap door, to an excavation dug by hand that extended the full length and breadth of the structure. Lake stone and river stone were used for the cellar walls and footings, except for the occasional more notable building wherein limestone was imported as ballast from Kingston.

Masonry for the fireplace was usually of brick, and this was either brought over by schooner from Oswego, New York, or purchased from a local brick works. Although there were very few early brick buildings, they became more commonplace towards the middle of the nineteenth century as local brick production began to grow. A small brick works was capable of producing up to a million bricks per year. The clay, usually blended with sand, was mixed with water to a mud-like consistency and poured into a brick-shaped mould. After drying on pallets out-of-doors in the good weather, they were set in a wood-fired kiln for burning.

The early bricks, in use up to the third quarter of the last century, were somewhat irregular in size, averaging less than 8″ × 4″ × 2″. They had flat surfaces but were often rough, warped, and frequently cracked. The bricks used in the last quarter of the century usually had a "frog" or depression in the bedding surface to create a better bond and were generally larger, measuring 8¼″ × 4″ × 2½″. Brick prices averaged four dollars a thousand at the kiln in the third quarter of the nineteenth century. Masons and bricklayers received the wage of fifteen cents per hour.

Lime used to make the mortar was produced by burning the timber from the cleared land. Heaped in piles and surmounted by a crown of fragmented limestone, the burning brush reduced the stone to a white powder. The burned lime, when placed in a trough of water, formed a thick putty. This paste mixed with sharp sand produced mortar for masonry work, plastering, or stucco finishing.

Apart from the fashionable desire for a clean, uncluttered building exterior, a stucco finish provided a jointless weather-resistant, low-maintenance finish. The incessant requirement of painting often caused the owner of a clapboard house to lay lath over the deteriorating weatherboards and to apply a coat of stucco. Consequently many of the older buildings in town are sheathed in two exterior coats.

Stucco was both troweled on and "thrown on." In the case of the latter, the mortar, somewhat wetter than usual, was scooped up on the back of the trowel and flung unceremoniously against the wall with a backhand motion. This roughcast and the pebble-dash method (wherein a quantity of small stones in the mortar mix provide a hard, decorative finish) reduced the likelihood of major cracking. Instead, a hair-like pattern of insignificant cracks around the individual stones eventually compensated for the settling of the building and the shrinking of the wooden structure underneath. Rather than painting, the surface was renewed by throwing on a thin coat — or spatterdash — of the original mixture.

Plaster usually contained a quantity of horse-hair within the mix to strengthen and serve as a binding agent. An item in shopkeeper Justus Williams' account book for the year 1834 records:

To 1 whitewash brush, 2 shillings, 6 pence; for lime furnished £1, 9 shillings, 3 pence; to hair furnished, 10 shillings, 7½ pence; to lime putty, 6 shillings; for contract of lathing and plastering, £ 21, 6 shillings, 1 pence.

Rather than being paid an hourly rate, plasterers were paid by the square yard covered, and they received less than five cents per square yard for each coat. The price of lime varied little over the years, and an advertisement in a local paper, dated November 3, 1876, for the *Oakville Tannery* reads: "Lime delivered to plasterers at manufacturers prices 20c per bushel. Strictly cash by the load."

Carpenters and joiners, who were more skilled carpenters capable of fine interior woodwork, received an average of a dollar and a half a day for their work. A helper received seventy-five cents. James McDonald notes in his Daybook in the year 1864: "Framing . . . framing a house 26 × 40, sills 6 × 10, joists framed into same, with a stringer framed in through centre, three butts, all studds nailed . . . 16 days at $1.50 including foundation . . . $24.00." Barter was also commonplace. Charles Sovereign of Bronte noted in his diary in the spring of 1845 that he traded "one door frame, three window frames, 36 lights of sash, all worth £ 1.39 for two black lambs."

Until the 1840s with the introduction of the circular saw, the mills around Oakville used an "up-and-down" saw, resulting in readily distinguishable vertical cut marks. Large beams were hand-adzed and timber framing was in common use in the construction of

The Most Wonderful Invention

dwellings until the middle of the century, and for barns until much later in the century. Timber framing involved fitting together of hewn timbers by mortise and tenon joints. Large wooden pegs were then hammered through the holes to secure the two parts. This method was replaced by "balloon framing" as nail factories increased production and saw mills produced more stock materials. The structural principles of this method were basically the same as timber framing, except that the mortise and tenon joint is replaced by a nailed joint. The timbers are slimmer and consequently more numerous. The result was an easier form of construction requiring less skill, less time, and less hand labour.

Early in the century, hand-split cedar shingles, often eighteen inches long, covered the roofs of the first houses. But as the century progressed, shingle factories appeared, as evidenced in the advertisement in the *Oakville Sentinel* of 1857: "Wanted, At the Oakville Shingle Factory, 500 cords shingle

timber — terms cash on delivery." In 1864, factory-made shingles were selling at $2.50 a thousand.

The earliest nails were produced from a square nail rod. The blacksmith cut the rod to the desired lengths, tapered all four sides to a point at one end and fashioned a round head at the other. Examples of this type of nail in the early construction of Oakville are rare. In his account book Justus Williams records: "December 5, 1833, 12 lb. of wrot nails six shillings, three pence; 5 lb. of cut nails eight pence — two shillings, one pence." By the time the town was under way, machine-cut nails were already available. Cut from a strip of iron, these nails were tapered throughout their length on two sides and were square-headed. Modifications of this method continued to bring about subtle changes in the appearance of nails produced in the third quarter of the century until wire nails were finally introduced at the beginning of the last quarter.

Although the finest hardwoods were readily

available, pine was the inevitable choice for flooring and trim woodwork. Invariably both were painted in the secondary rooms and often in the front rooms as well. In the front rooms, pine trim and pine doors were often times masterfully grained to give the appearance of finer wood. This practice grew in the middle of the century to become quite fashionable, as did the use of darker colours. Originally white lead and whitewash were the most common colours for exterior and interior, although Justus Williams mentions the availability of "Yellow Oker, Prussian Blue, Indigo, Venetian Red and Turkey Umber." Dark Green was the ever-popular favourite for shutter blinds, and George Sumner records in his diary a turn-of-the-century recipe: "ingredients for green paint for blinds; 2 lbs. of Imperial green, 1 lb. Paris green, 1 lb. white lead. Boiled oil."

As paint colours grew darker so did wall coverings and the use of wall coverings with bolder, heavier designs. In 1893, paper hanger and painter William Forrester charged George Sumner fifteen cents a roll for the eleven rolls required to paper his sitting room and five cents a yard for the ceiling border. The introduction of black horse-hair stuffed furniture and heavy window hangings aided the dark and ominous appearance of many Victorian rooms. Fortunately, as the decorating trends leaned to the darker side, the increased availability of large window glass brought about the use of larger window openings.

Windows are divided by glazing bars into panes, and the number of panes per sash is a fairly accurate gauge as to the age of a building. Of course, one must take into account

the common practice of modernizing, whereby the sash may be many times updated as larger glass sections became available. Early glass was made in small panes to facilitate transportation as well as manufacture, so a division of four or five panes in width usually indicates a structure earlier than 1820. This glass, with its slight bluish tint, was pocked with flaws and often warped. In 1834, Justus Williams noted the frequent sale of glass in 8″ × 10″ panes and occasionally 7″ × 9″. By 1835 the division of windows into three panes in width was quite common. James McDonald recorded in 1864 the purchase of three panes of glass 12″ × 16″ from Mr. Orr, a paint and glass merchant, for the sum of twenty-five cents. The availability of larger sheets brought about the division of sash into two panes by 1870, and by 1890 double-hung windows were often one sheet of glass each.

The average house in early Oakville was a modest dwelling that over the years acquired various additions. As the needs and means of the inhabitants grew, so did their houses. Consequently a collection of woodsheds, hen houses, root houses, stables, privies, and wells dotted the back yards. These back yards were usually enclosed by a solid plank fence to confine livestock, while a white picket fence often enclosed a front-door garden. All available land was cultivated for vegetable gardens and fruit trees.

In 1867 a storey-and-a-half, well-finished brick house, 32′ × 26′, with a kitchen tail and a cellar, cost in the neighbourhood of $1,500. However, with a mortgage rate of ten percent, fire insurance a must, a determined tax collector at the door, and an average annual income well under five hundred dollars, the nineteenth-century home owner had little money to spare.

The rapid growth of the town is illustrated in the records of the time. In 1836, Thomas Rolph, in his *Statistical Account of Upper Canada*, noted "the village has increased so rapidly that it now extends across the creek—it was formerly on the left bank—and a good draw bridge is erected over it." The Assessment Rolls record an increase from fifty homeowners in 1840 to eighty-three in 1843. According to the Census of 1841, Oakville supported fourteen carpenters and consisted of seventy occupied premises. However, by 1851 there were twenty-seven carpenters and a population of 916. Oakville listed four log houses, 130 frame houses, and just four brick houses at that time. *The Sentinel* in 1857 claimed that the town had doubled in population in three years, and the Census of 1861 reflected this growth by listing the same four log buildings but also 228 frame dwellings and forty-five brick houses.

The port of Oakville grew rapidly during the 1830s and commerce flourished during the forties, but it was the fifties that produced the greatest building boom Oakville had experienced. During the 1850s the greatest proportion of early buildings that now constitute "Old Oakville" were erected, and this uneven chronological distribution is reflected in the main part of the text of this book. Soon after the Village of Oakville became the Town of Oakville in 1857, the *Canada Directory* of 1857-58 published the following description:

"An incorporated Town in the Township of Trafalgar, County of Halton, etc. . . . which

13

forms an excellent and land-locked harbor, of easy access. Oakville is advantageously situated for shipbuilding purposes, and a number of first-class vessels are built here every year. It is the outlet for the shipping of flour and other products to the American side, besides being the wheat market of the County of Halton. The station of the Great Western Railway is on the outskirt of the town. Daily mail, population about 2000.''

In 1855 *The Sentinel* published a curious announcement that must have surely sparked the hopes of many a wishful tenant:

''Now is the time to secure a Homestead. Grand Lottery of Four Convenient dwelling Houses and valuable lots. Tickets only $2.00. To the young men of Oakville and surrounding country this will prove a rare opportunity to obtain a house or other valuable property by investing a small amount! The winners of the Dwellings to pay $25 cash. The Dwelling houses and lots contained in the above list are owned by J. J. Hilberd and are situated in the flourishing village of Oakville, on the west side of the Sixteen Mile Creek, being a cluster of neat residences, admired by all for the beauty of their location, and the substantial and neat appearance of the buildings, which are new and finished in the latest style of architecture, with every convenience for a comfortable home.''

Five basic styles influenced the domestic and commercial architecture of old Oakville. These styles overlapped one another, as several were fashionable at any one time, and, of course, there were adaptations of these styles many years after they were in vogue. The Georgian style of architecture grew out of

eighteenth-century Britain and blossomed in the Thirteen Colonies. By 1827, when Oakville was founded, only remnants of the Georgian concept remained to leave an impression on the north shore of Lake Ontario. The Georgian house was a solid, sturdily constructed rectangle. It was one, one-and-a-half, two, and even two-and-a-half storeys in height. The number of windows was rigidly balanced around a centre door and central hall. The broad, six-panel door was usually embellished by an overhead, half-circle light or a rectangular transom light and occasionally a pair of side lights to illuminate the hall. The window in the second storey above the doorway was often given to a more elaborate decoration than the others. The roof was of a steep pitch and heavy, blocky chimneys mounted the gable ends. The cornice was narrow and boldly sculptured with small dentils or bracket blocks as an added refinement. There was a disciplined symmetry in the design.

The beginning of the nineteenth century saw the introduction of a new form of architecture in Upper Canada. Again this style originated in Britain, where it was called ''Adam,'' but as it spread to the United States it came to be known as ''Federal.'' Internationally, the style may be called ''Neo-Classic,'' and because the Loyalists and their children carried the design elements to this part of the country, it is often described as ''Loyalist Neo-Classic.'' This restrained, harmonious form was an outgrowth of a new interest in the classical worlds of Pompeii and Rome. It introduced lightness of scale and delicacy in texture and colour to domestic architecture. Neo-Classic structures were dignified, eleg-

ant, and very precise. The Neo-Classic style marked the end of the steep roof and block chimneys. It heralded the arrival of the ellipse as a design element and the implementation of slender pilasters and the use of refined exterior and interior trim. The horizontal lines of clapboard siding that covered the frame house were now thought to be disturbing to the eye and stucco became the common surface finish. The balanced window placement and central doorway remained, but other features such as a wide elliptical arch in the entrance hall and a spiral staircase became fashionable. Elements of the Neo-Classic style are some of the most common design features of early Oakville.

With the influx of Colonists from Britain who rushed into the fledgling community, yet another style appeared to meld with the increasing number of dwellings already being erected. This new group of settlers included many professional men of means who had travelled to other parts of the world; men who were fired with enthusiasm and full of new ideas. They were men of taste and they intended to build homes, shops, and offices to suit their tastes. They had little desire to conform with the existing fashions, and they chose to build in a romantic if not entirely practical style. These builders of the Regency era incorporated the verandah and large casement windows in their dwellings so they might enjoy the surrounding landscape of this new land. Roofs became lower in pitch over a central rectangular block of a house. These houses were often a storey or a storey-and-a-half in height and assumed a low profile even with their tall, sometimes decorative chimneys. Stucco and pebbledash was a common exterior finish so there would be little distraction to the composition and pattern of the ornamental treillage that often decorated the long, low verandahs. The Regency influence is evident in several large Oakville homes, but many of the smaller cottages better express the form.

At the same time as the Regency style was gaining in popularity, there were also influences from what is known as the Classical Revival or Greek Revival style. This form grew out of a renewed interest in classical architecture in both Europe and America. Oakville had few examples of the Greek Revival style and even fewer exist today. Although it gained great acceptance in the United States, the style was felt to be extremely unyielding and unsympathetic as a domestic architectural form in this part of the world. The tall columns and crowning pediments, typical of the style, were too costly for a modest private dwelling and were thought to be suitable for only large public buildings. Full Revival architecture displayed classical columns, pilasters, entablatures, and architraves, but even so several local buildings incorporated the basic Temple plan with front and rear gables.

The next architectural phase to leave its mark on Oakville was not one singular style but rather many different expressions. Collectively called ''Victorian,'' this romantic Revival style encompasses Gothic, Tudor, Italianate, and Picturesque forms. In the Victorian age, cottages assumed the guise of castles and large homes adopted the characteristics of modest cottages. The rectangle and square plan gave way to the ''cross,'' ''T,'' ''L,'' and ''H'' plans. Consequently, gables became very evident and dormers sprang through the roofs. Decorative bargeboards appeared on the eaves. Pointed arch windows lit the gable walls. Roofs again became steeper, walls higher, and eaves overhung further. To support the eaves, brackets increased in size and complexity. Towers, turrets, bay windows, arches, paired windows, balconies, and verandahs all added to the Picturesque look.

Patterned brickwork and heavy woodwork created a busy appearance leading to an eventual overindulgence that gradually caused a degeneracy in style. The sense of proportion was disappearing rapidly as the century progressed, and frantic attempts to retain a semblance of order were demonstrated in the ''Carpenter Gothic'' fantasies of the last years of the nineteenth century. Poorly designed, factory-made products were evidenced in the mechanical fretwork of the late Victorian bargeboards that overtook the early handwork, and the final result was the total demise of design and quality.

Oakville is a microcosm of early Ontario architecture. Each architectural style to appear in Ontario in the nineteenth century is characterized in the building of this town. Rarely, however, are the styles represented in their purest form, and it is perhaps best to accept them as vernacular adaptations of the classical modes. For, after all, the domestic and commercial buildings illustrated in this book are the homes and shops where people actually lived and worked—our grandparents, our great grandparents and their parents. This book is a tribute to our predecessors and an acknowledgement of their most personal legacy—the place they called home.

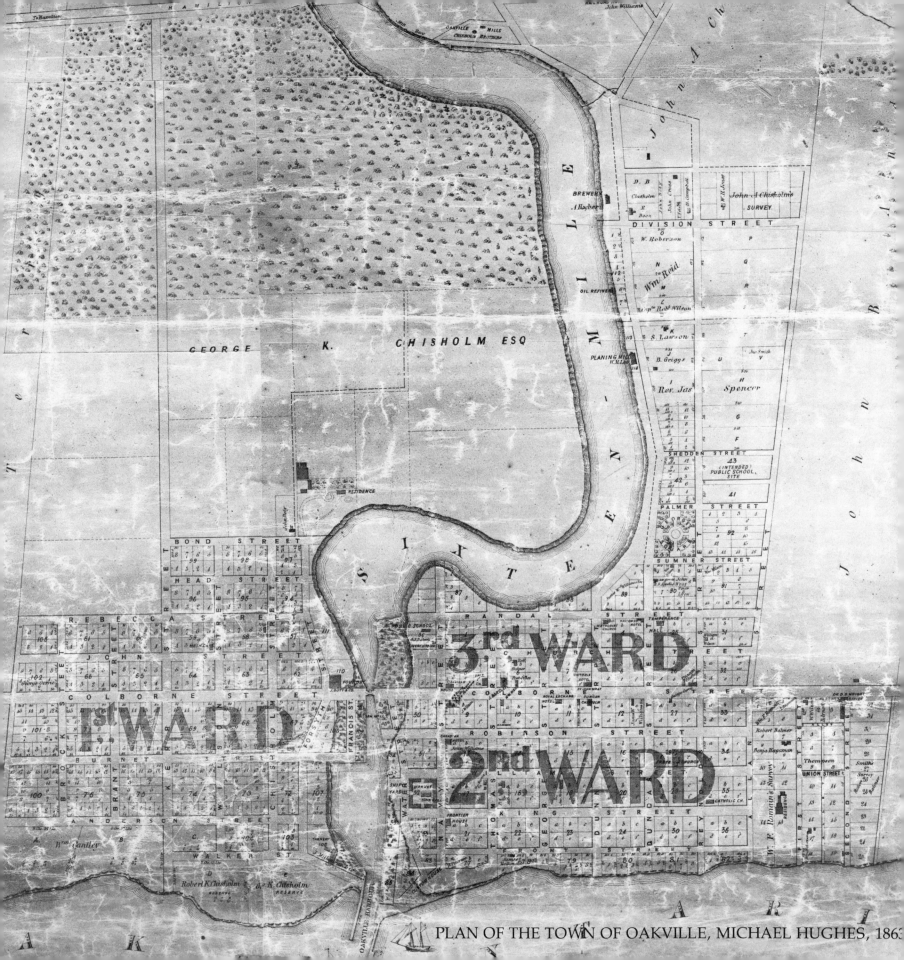

PLAN OF THE TOWN OF OAKVILLE, MICHAEL HUGHES, 1863

THE BUILDINGS

The buildings that will be examined in detail in the main part of this text have been selected as representative of the architectural styles that influenced the shape of the town. Each structure has either managed to retain its original character with a minimum of alteration or successfully adopted the style of a later period modification. The majority of the structures stand within the boundaries of the original townsite. However, several exceptions have been made to demonstrate the full range of architectural influences. These buildings are now within the boundaries of the Town of Oakville.

For the purpose of clarity, the authors have chosen to refer to streets by their present nomenclature, as many of the street names marked on early maps are no longer in use. Highway No. 5 was originally known as The Dundas Street, and Trafalgar Road was similarly designated Dundas Street. Colborne Street is now renamed Lakeshore Road, as is the old Lake Shore Road. The authors have also made the generalization that the lake front and Lakeshore Road run east and west and that all cross streets run north and south.

Circa 1829
The Merrick Thomas House

LAKESIDE PARK

For over one hundred and twenty-five years the Thomas House stood on the site of Purdue High School. White pine, cut off what is now St. Jude's cemetery, was roughly adzed to twelve inches square and laid as a sill on a foundation of stones gathered from the newly cleared fields. Upon this a frame of lesser timbers was raised and secured in place with hardwood pegs. Unskinned pine logs were used as joists, while others were drawn down to the sawmill on the Sixteen. There they were cut into boards and then drawn back up again to serve as sheathing, planking, and interior trim to complete one of Oakville's earliest pioneer homesteads.

Structures similar to the Thomas House were erected in the Thirteen Colonies to replace the first log cabins, and in many cases the Loyalists continued to build in this fashion upon their arrival in Upper Canada. Therefore, it is no surprise to learn that Merrick Thomas was born in Vermont in 1803. He migrated with his family as a child in 1810, but by the tender age of nine he was left to fend for himself. Working as a store clerk, sawyer, and sailor, Merrick rapidly acquired a multitude of talents. Thus in 1827, when approached by William Chisholm to assume the responsibilities of laying out the new townsite of Oakville, he was well-equipped to accept. Merrick's new wife, Esther, a sister-in-law of William Chisholm, ran the 200-acre farm, while the closest he came to farming was to acquire a thrashing mill. Remaining very much the businessman, Thomas assumed numerous civic positions of

responsibility and trust in the new community. As he prospered, the farmhouse was enlarged by an addition of such proportion that the original structure became a much-altered back kitchen.

Merrick Thomas died in 1856, and Esther continued to live on at the farm until her death in 1891, whereupon the property was passed to their son, Murray. In 1951 Murray Hill Farm, as it was known, was sold to the Department of National Defence. In 1955, the old farmhouse was sold to the Oakville Historical Society for $1.60, and the original section was moved to its present location in Lakeside Park on land deeded to the town by Mrs. Hazel Mathews and her sister Dr. Juliet Chisholm.

Windows had been filled in with cupboards, doors cut into the wainscoting, the ceiling lowered three times, and the large fireplace closed up. With great care to retain the original material, both the interior and exterior were exactingly reconstructed and restored. The Norfolk latch on the main door must be similar to the ones Justus Williams stocked in 1837 and sold for one shilling threepence. The Suffolk latch on the garret door also remains unchanged since the house was built. A proud testimony to the HL hinges on which it still hangs, this straight and sturdy door was the sole entry to the loft where the Thomas children slept. Downstairs, Merrick and Esther enjoyed the privacy of an eight-foot-square sliproom, the only room division in the building. The blocky stone chimney is visible for just half its height on the outside

wall. This was not an infrequent feature in small dwellings of the period, as it retained the chimney within the structure to conserve heat, yet permitted the chimney to project through the exterior wall affording greater interior space. Only four of their seven children survived childhood, but these four, all boys, must surely have shivered when it came time to retire on a blustery winter's night. The only heat for the loft was provided by the chimney breast.

A visit inside this sixteen by twenty-four foot building will help one appreciate only too well the desire of the Thomas family for more space. The Thomas House, a companion building to the Old Post Office Museum, is maintained by the Oakville Historical Society.

THOMAS HOUSE
1829

Circa 1834
The Peter McCorquodale House

143 FRONT STREET

Peter McCorquodale, a Scotsman, twenty-three years of age, his Irish bride, Elizabeth, and their infant son arrived in the port of Oakville in 1830. With the first sale of town lands in July of 1833, McCorquodale purchased two lots, commanding a fine view of the harbour and a great sweep of the lake. On the southerly lot he had built a timber frame and clapboard dwelling. It has been suggested this house may have originally comprised just three bays. If so, it is quite possible the structure received a coat of pebbledash stucco when the westerly two bays were added. When completed, the building consisted of four upstairs bedrooms with a kitchen tail at the rear. For sixty-five years it was in the possession of the McCorquodale family.

McCorquodale, a much-respected mariner, captained the schooner *Royal Tar* of which he was a part owner. When he died of "protracted illness" in 1850 at age forty-three, the *Oakville Sun* noted his demise with the poetic epitaph: "After sailing through this tempestuous world with ardour and integrity, he has cast anchor in that haven from whence no traveller returneth."

Seven children survived him, and of his four sons, three followed their father in his love of ships by becoming ship's masters. One of the sons, James, however, forsook the tradition of sail by later becoming a steamer captain.

Peter McCorquodale was one of the founding members of the Presbyterian Congregation in Oakville, and both he and his family were active and devout church people. When his daughter Rebecca moved from Oakville, she was presented with a silver tea service as a parting gift from the congregation. Peter's wife Elizabeth died in 1866, but the house remained in the McCorquodale family until 1899, when their daughter, Elizabeth Jane, and her husband, W. H. Ballard, who was a Public School Inspector in Hamilton, sold the two lots to John A. Chisholm Jr. for $1,500.

Chisholm consolidated the two lots with property he had acquired across Front Street in what is now Lakeside Park. He and his brother Charles were very successful in the development of a pea-shelling machine in the United States, and John built "Mount Vernon," an elegant gambrel-roofed summer estate house on these lakefront lots. McCorquodale's old house served as quarters for the gardener and groom, and the surrounding grounds soon included a gambrel-roofed stable and coach house, a greenhouse, a gazebo, and carefully manicured gardens.

Unfortunately, Chisholm died four years later. Mount Vernon became the home of a movie studio and was shortly thereafter destroyed by fire. The land parcels became separated and the lakeside portion was possessed by the Town for arrears of taxes. The old McCorquodale house became a sad and empty derelict.

In 1933 Frank Pullen bought the two original lots from Chisholm's widow for his daughter Gwyneth and her husband Ralph Young, who after renting for some time were given the property. The accompanying sketch depicts the house as it looked without the three pleasantly disposed dormers that were added in 1934. At the same time the gable end chimneys were removed and a sturdy single chimney and fireplace were installed. The pebbledash finish has been renewed with a later stucco surface, just as the window sash has been modernized at some time. Several sympathetic additions have been made to the east and to the original summer kitchen in the rear in order to create a sculpture studio for Mrs. Young.

The cornice, bargeboards, and window surrounds are virtually devoid of visual interest, but this simplicity of design and scarcity of detail only strengthens the impressive doorcase. Here, the joiner's sense of proportion and woodworking skills are displayed in a broad, expansive work of art. A bold, projecting cornice and a high frieze are supported by four fluted pilasters. Over each pilaster a delicate diamond shape further embellishes the entry. The eight-panel door fashioned faithfully after the original is surrounded by sidelights of five panes each to illuminate the central entrance hall. All but one glass is original. The broken pane bore a date that probably was scratched in Peter McCorquodale's own hand — "1834."

Circa 1835
The Old Post Office Museum

LAKESIDE PARK

During the first seven years of Oakville's existence, the townspeople relied on the delivery of mail from a post office at Trafalgar Road and Highway No. 5. The mail was carried between there and the town by horseback and it was only with the population growth of the mid-thirties that the establishment of a post office in Oakville seemed necessary.

In 1835, a twenty-four foot, six-inch square structure was erected high on the bank of the Sixteen on the west side of Navy Street below Lakeshore Road. Among his many other civic duties, William Chisholm was appointed to the position of Postmaster. Although he had held that title for ten years at the Nelson Post Office, it was his son, R. K. Chisholm as Deputy Postmaster, who assumed most of the responsibility. There was little, however, that he could do to resolve the problems because the postal service was in a frightful state. Still under the control of the British Government, postage rates were excessively high and stamps and envelopes were non-existent. Instead, letters were folded in half and sealed with wax. Often as not letters were sent collect, leaving the collection of tariff up to the harried postmaster. In the early years, elections were held in the post office, the vote being taken by a show of hands. Unfortunately there was often a display of fisticuffs outside afterwards. The building also doubled as the headquarters for the company administering the plank road from Oakville to Fergus.

In 1849 the provinces finally gained control of the mails from the Crown and consequently were able to reduce the rates by one-third. Two years later, Canada's first postage stamp was introduced, and in the same year a contract was let out to carry the mails by stage along the Lake Shore Road between Toronto and Hamilton. In the summer months the steamer *Magnet* brought the mail into the Port of Oakville. The *Semi-Weekly Sentinel* was in the habit of periodically carrying a "List of Letters" wherein alphabetical lists of names were printed in the hope that the intended recipient would see his name. The little post office gained greater prominence in 1855 when the Great Western Railway assumed the role of mail carrier and it fell upon the Oakville office to dispatch the bags to Trafalgar and Bronte Post Offices. With these additional requirements, a fast-growing community and the limited facilities of the small building, the Post Office was moved in 1856, under the hand of Postmaster Robert Balmer, to new larger premises.

For most of the next hundred years, the little building suffered a multitude of uses. It was blackened with the soot and grime of a blacksmith's shop and tainted with years of service as a stable. In the late 1920s Percy Bath put an extension on the southwest wall to accommodate a lengthy cabin cruiser he was building in the old Post Office. The building later sheltered a welding business and for many years was a storehouse for a tannery. It was during this period that a second storey was added to the structure, and quite likely the cupola was incorporated as a ventilator on the roof at this time.

When the tannery changed hands, the building was given in trust to Hazel Mathews. Mrs. Mathews was a pioneer in her efforts to preserve a part of Oakville's history, and under her guidance and with little help the building was moved in 1950 to its present site in Lakeside Park. There, after meticulous reconstruction, it again took on the outward appearance of the old Post Office. The second storey was removed and the roof reinstated on the original plate, the pins fitting back into

the original holes. Twenty-foot, four-by-twelve planks, held together by a loose tongue-joint and dove-tailed at the corners, make up the walls. Although most of the material is original to the structure, the new porch pillars were patterned after those of the 1833 Justice Williams shop. The door and window sash were salvaged from the demolition of a contemporary building, the James Appelbe brick store built in the 1840s on the southeast corner of Trafalgar Road and Highway No. 5. The building, which served for many years as the Trafalgar Township Hall, was demolished in 1949. Beneath the wooden shingles of the old Post Office tin sheathing still exists.

Under the jurisdiction of the Oakville Historical Society, which was formed to administer the Old Post Office Museum, the building has found new life displaying the artifacts of old Oakville.

Circa 1835
The David Patterson House

19 NAVY STREET

A granddaughter of David Patterson wrote the following family history: "My great grandfather, David Patterson, lived in Ballymena, County Antrim, Ireland. His ancestors were Scotch who had gone to Ireland with some two or three hundred families about 1600. David Patterson married — Chambers, and they had four children, William, James, Nancy and David, the youngest, my grandfather, born in 1807. When only a boy my Grandfather started to learn his trade as carpenter and cabinet builder in Belfast, a distance of fourteen miles or more from Ballymena. Once a month it was his privilege to come home to visit his parents. Grandfather's older brother James and sister Nancy came to Canada while Grandfather was still learning his trade, and on completion of his apprenticeship at the age of eighteen or nineteen, he came to Canada.

Greatgrandmother was born in North Carolina. Her maiden name was Polly McCarther (or McArthur). Her father was a slave owner, but before emancipation liberated his slaves and moved to New Jersey. Here Polly married George Griggs. They journeyed to Canada during the latter part of the 18th century or beginning of the 19th century, going first to Dundas, but later settling on a farm of one hundred acres, just east of Oakville. Two brothers of Greatgrandfather's Benjamin and Barnett Griggs, came over from the States about the same time, all being of U.E. Loyalist stock."

Polly and George Griggs had two sons and six daughters, and one of them, Agnes, married David Patterson. By 1827, David was employed at William Chisholm's shipyard as a shipwright, but soon he turned his carpentry skills to the building of houses in the rapidly expanding community, and in 1834 he purchased, from Chisholm, the lot at the corner of Navy and Front Streets. He built the two-and-a-half storey clapboard house

shortly thereafter, and it was in this house that the Pattersons raised their eight children; George, David, James, Robert, Agnes Mary, Samuel, Cyrus John (a carpenter like his father), and Matilda Jane. The Census of 1851 records that David Patterson also maintained a "carpenter shop" on the premises.

In 1866 the Collector's Rolls indicate that David Patterson purchased two additional lots directly to the south of his home in what is now Lakeside Park. By the following year the increase in assessment suggests that a house, somewhat smaller than 19 Navy Street, was erected on one of the lots, and that he moved into it, renting out 19 Navy Street to James Andrew and Oliver Buck. David Patterson continued in his profession and was recorded as late as the Census of 1871 as a carpenter. He died in 1877 and his wife Agnes died in 1884. George Sumner recorded in his diary on March 24, 1886: "The Old David Patterson Property was sold today by auction. The whole place brought $1620." This price may have included the other lots.

19 Navy Street was purchased by Josephine Milbourne, a spinster who had been renting the property since 1873. Shortly after the purchase, the house received major renovations in the form of a brick veneer, decorative fish-scale shingles on the gables, a new doorway, a bay, and two balconies, in order to bring it in line with the Victorian taste. Josephine left the property in 1929 to her niece who within two years sold it. The house has changed hands several times since, and numerous additions have been made to the tail, but the basic spirit of the structure has not been altered.

The Patterson House is built on a centre hall plan with a dining room on the right and a parlour on the left. The dining room is blessed with a charming, unusually small four-

by-three-foot mantel with an iron grate and hood which was in all likelihood installed by the Milbournes. The living room has, as its focal point, a large 6'6" wide mantelpiece of a delicate Adam design, while an even larger mantel, standing 5'2" high and 7'6" long, dominates the bedroom above.

The parlour mantel is flanked by a deep bay and a pair of French doors that lead to a verandah on the north wall. Although the windows on the front of the house appear to be of a six-over-six pane design, they are actually a grid of muntins affixed to a large piece of glass in a bid to restore the window sash from the turn of the century style to that of an earlier period.

A simple chair rail surrounds the parlour, the dining room and the main bedroom. The handsome staircase with well-turned balusters is further enhanced by a cranberry globe fitted with a brass collar that crowns the newel post, to supposedly signify a fully paid mortgage. The pine floorboards of the David Patterson House range up to twenty-six inches in width, and the unsquared planks are alternately arranged to utilize the natural tapering widths.

It has been said that during the nineteenth century the David Patterson House had at one time been a boarding school for girls and at another time an inn. In either case, the chair rails in the three principal rooms could thus be accounted for. Although it would be pure supposition, Oliver Buck, who rented the house during the 1860s, had relatives who operated a tavern in Trafalgar Township, and Oliver may have converted the Patterson House into a hotel.

Circa 1837
The James McDonald House

176 FRONT STREET

When he arrived in Oakville to work on the erection of the piers, James McDonald of Aberlour in north-eastern Scotland was already a well-seasoned carpenter. Here he was to excel as a builder of graceful, well-proportioned buildings, his own home exemplifying some of the finest Neo-Classic characteristics in all Oakville.

In 1837 McDonald bought two waterfront lots for the sum of £100 from a fellow carpenter, James McPherson. On the westerly lot, McDonald erected, on a lakestone foundation, a timber frame, two-storey dwelling. According to the Presbyterian records, James McDonald and his wife had three children. Both boys were to learn the trade of carpentry and joinery from their skilled father. Peter relocated in Ridgetown, but James McDonald Jr. remained in Oakville to work with his elder, forming a business partnership with him and eventually operating a planing mill. When the Canada Presbyterian Church on William Street was completed in 1850, James McDonald Senior was entitled to much of the credit for its construction. Even later in life, McDonald worked on the new Market building, or Town Hall, as it was referred to in the Daybook he and his son kept.

There are indications from an Assessment Roll of the year 1873 that McDonald, then eighty-two years of age, no longer requiring the entire house, duplexed and rented out a portion of it. Seven years later he died and three years after his death his wife died, leaving the house in the possession of their

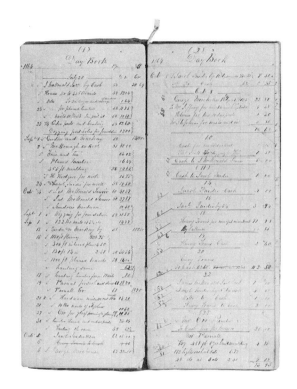

daughter Catherine, or Miss Kate as she was called. Miss Kate continued to rent out a portion of the house to summer visitors for many years. She eventually became very ill over a prolonged period, the house deteriorated, and her estate sold the property in 1939 to a widow, Mrs. Ella Gibbons of Toronto.

The building underwent considerable renovation in the two years that Mrs. Gibbons owned the property, including a one-storey addition to the west, a garage to the east, and

a wide room extending across the rear of the building that provided a dramatic view of the lake. In 1941 the house was sold, only to change owners again in five years' time. However, since 1946 the McDonald House has remained in the hands of the Dunlop Stewarts, and it is endowed with a glow gained from long-time affection.

The stucco exterior finish on this well-proportioned frame dwelling and the flanking chimneys rising within the gable walls both serve to underscore the symmetry of the imposing ten-bay façade. Although the shutter blinds and hangers are original, twentieth-century sash has replaced the originals in all but the upper rear windows, where a six-over-six fenestration still contains the original panes. The uncluttered cornice and clean sweeping returns are light in scale, and their stark lines enhance the delicate woodwork exhibited in the doorway. This classic entry, with its finely edged cornice, deep frieze, fluted pilasters, and sidelights frame an unusual eight-panel door. The inside of the door displays eight recessed panels, whereas the exterior shows only the upper four to be recessed while the lower four are merely incised. Sturdy, early hardware secures the main doors as well as many of the interior six-panel and tongue-and-groove doors. One of these still bears a handsome Norfolk latch, proof that good design and good workmanship, as exemplified in the McDonald house, are forever functional and forever fashionable.

Circa 1838
The John Moore House

29 NAVY STREET

John Moore was born in 1806 in County Armagh in the north of Ireland and there he was schooled for the Presbyterian ministry. However, during his passage to Upper Canada as a young immigrant, he developed a keen interest in ships and acquired the rudiments of navigation from the captain of the vessel. Upon his arrival in Oakville, Moore found employment as a bookkeeper at Richard Coates' sawmill. It was Coates who later prompted Moore to get into the shipping business by pointing out the economics and subsequently the handsome profits to be made by owning one's own ship. Moore contracted construction of a four-masted schooner of 180 tons, and by 1834 the *John Mackenzie* and its eight-man crew had begun its travels up and down the lake. In 1837 John Moore and several fellow Orangemen from Oakville were among the raiding party that torched the steamer *Caroline* and sent her to her destruction over the British side of Niagara Falls as a symbol of patriotic righteousness. Their bid to stop William Lyon Mackenzie and his "provisional government" was successful, but the incident created sufficient controversy to keep Moore in the north country until the situation cooled down. In 1834 John Moore had purchased the lot at Navy and King Streets, and it is supposed that he had the dwelling built there in 1838 upon his return to Oakville. Here, he and his wife Sally, daughter of Barnett Griggs, an early settler, made their home. In 1839 their son Barnett Griggs Moore was born. John was one of several adventurous and enterprising men who invested in the Oakville Hydraulic Company. In 1840 Moore sold the house to his father-in-law and in all probability used the monies derived from the sale to invest in the ill-fated venture. Moore took

heavy losses when the company failed in 1841, but three years later he suffered an even greater loss when his young, twenty-six-year-old wife died.

Barnett Griggs retained the property, letting it out to various tenants over the years. Being an old hotelier of some note (he was the owner and operator of the Halfway House just east of Oakville) he saw the possibilities of the advantageous location and enlarged the structure considerably, converting it into a hotel. Joseph Belyea leased the "Frontier House" in 1853 and advertised "the largest and his accommodations as the best in Oakville. He spared no expense in fitting up his house for their reception. Coaches always in attendance to convey passengers to and from boats." Because of the proximity to the landing and because the clientele was largely comprised of passengers from the boats, the Frontier House soon became known as the "Steamboat Hotel." Reuben Brooks took over the proprietorship two years later and in the *Oakville Sentinel* advertised the hotel as a "popular resort for boarders." By 1860 the structure again reverted to a private home, and with the death of Griggs and his wife Christeen the house was sold in 1870 to Robert Appelbe.

Robert Swanton Appelbe, son of Squire Appelbe, was a prominent barrister and solicitor who established a practice in Oakville during the 1860s. His wife, Eliza, was a daughter of Thomas Joffray Robertson, the first Headmaster of the new Normal School in Toronto. The Appelbes had six children and for seventy years the John Moore House remained in the hands of the Appelbe family. By 1916, with most of the family gone, the house was much larger than required. Consequently

when a neighbour offered to purchase a portion of the structure, a deal was quickly made and the northerly end was sawn off and sold for $400. It was moved around the corner to a lot on King Street, set upon a new foundation and a verandah erected on two sides. Finally in 1941 Kathleen Appelbe, a spinster, sold the old John Moore House.

Under examination it is revealed that the remaining structure was not built at one time. It appears as if it was originally a half-house consisting of four bays; a door and window on the ground floor and two windows on the second storey. The structure was originally sheathed in clapboard and given its rough-cast stucco finish when the second or third addition was made. A tail at the rear containing a back staircase was probably added at the time of conversion to a hotel and seems to have come from an older structure, drawn up and affixed to the main body of the house. The original window sash on the main part of the dwelling is long gone. The present window break-up of eight-over-eight panes is in reality a two-over-two configuration from the turn of the century with additional muntins cut into the frame. This attempt to recapture the grace of the building's earlier days was pleasantly carried out by the Manbert family who succeeded the Appelbes.

Although the Frontier House is but two-thirds of what it once was, it is twice the house it was originally to be, yet the building still manages to maintain a well-proportioned dignity. The somewhat asymmetrical window and door arrangement on the façade only adds to its character, lending just the slightest suggestion that there is more of a story behind the John Moore House than meets the eye.

Circa 1839
The Melancthon Simpson House

235 TRAFALGAR ROAD

In November of 1838 William Chisholm sold this sixth of an acre lot to William Dolby. Dolby held onto the land for six years whereupon he and his wife sold to Owen Murphy. After two years Murphy sold the property in 1846 to Melancthon Simpson, who at twenty-three was soon to be married. It is believed that it was Dolby who commissioned the house to be built on the land and that it was built by John Potter as one of a pair of houses he built at the time. Potter's house on a neighbouring lot was subsequently destroyed by fire in 1869 but, supposedly, like the house at 235 Trafalgar Road, it incorporated many construction techniques common to ship-building. Both Potter and Simpson were noted ship-wrights and each was capable of executing the workmanship involved. Simpson himself could have built the house in the two years prior to his marriage. However, the building bears strong similarities to other Regency cottages erected during the mid-1830s in other sections of the province.

The Census taken in 1851 records Melancthon Simpson as a Wesleyan Methodist born in Upper Canada in 1823. In 1848 he married Esther Louisa Terry, daughter of Elizabeth Silverthorn and the Eton-educated John Terry. A daughter Elizabeth was born to the Simpsons in 1849 at their cottage on what was then called Dundas Street. About that time Melancthon and his brother John purchased a shipyard and commenced building the first of many illustrious schooners under the Simpson name. Their ships, identified by gay stripes and finely carved, brightly painted figureheads, were highly admired. The Simpson brothers built vessels in Bronte, Wellington Square, and other neighbouring ports in addition to Oakville. Their ships ranged from the 141-ton *Lily* to the 230-ton *Sea Gull,* and between the years 1852 and 1861 there are records of the Simpsons build-

ing at least twelve ships. As steel-hulled ships grew in popularity, the brothers closed down their activities in Oakville to pursue successful careers as builders of these new ships in Toronto and other lake ports.

In 1858 Melancthon and Esther sold their cottage to James Worts "upon certain trusts." However, in 1866 the title reverted to Simpson who resold the property a year later to James Newlands. The Newlands held the land for fifteen years and sold the house and the lot behind, with a barn to John Freestone Jr. in 1882. John Freestone worked at the Oakville Basket Factory and as a young man he handed his earnings over to his mother to put aside for him. By the time he was twenty, John had saved $525 and with this he paid cash for the home he bought for his new bride Mary Bowerbank. Here the Freestones raised their daughter, Grace, now Mrs. Wilfrid S. Hall, who recalls that in 1915 they moved into the new house that her father had built on the property to the east, facing on Reynolds Street. In 1920 Freestone sold the house on Trafalgar Road to Faith Robinson, who was a member of the Chisholm family. At the time of their marriage in 1938, the house became the property of the present owners, Mr. and Mrs. C. D. Chisholm.

The Melancthon Simpson House is the earliest-known example of Regency design existing in Oakville. The hipped-roof cottage and the tent-shaped verandah roof readily identify the style. The verandah at one time sheltered the casement windows and bordered the house on three sides. Sufficient woodwork remains to indicate the skill involved in creating the fanciful treillage. The casement windows on the front façade and the southerly side of the Simpson House are embellished with fluted surrounds to complement the fluted pilasters of the front door architrave. The broad door is most distinctive

because of the two very heavily moulded panels, but perhaps the most interesting feature of the entry is the ingenious method whereby the builder inserted two sidelights to illuminate the central hall. The hall is narrow, no more than four feet wide, but as it approaches the main entry it curves back to accommodate a six-foot-wide doorcase.

This one-storey frame dwelling is constructed of timber framing with diagonal-braced corners on 10" × 10", hand-hewn sills 24½ feet and 30½ feet in length. Similarly in the attic, outside plates, divided by joists, run the length of the structure. Carlings (a nautical term to describe "short pieces of timber ranging fore and aft from one deck beam to another") are mortised into the joists as under the deck of a ship. The exterior is sheathed in untapered weatherboards laid over planks ranging in width from eight to twenty inches.

The building was originally a centre-hall plan with an asymmetrical room arrangement. The centre hall has been shortened, an interior wall of a later vintage removed, and door openings relocated. However, the owners have meticulously reproduced the original wood trim. Similarly on the exterior, a building which had been drawn up and attached to the rear was enlarged in the 1950s with a sizeable addition, but the Melancthon Simpson House has retained its pleasing proportions.

Circa 1840
O'Reilly's Tavern

152 LAKESHORE ROAD EAST

The land on which this building now stands passed through the hands of numerous members of the Chisholm family. In 1834 William Chisholm sold it to James King who turned it over to his brother William McKenzie King (both being wards of William Chisholm). In 1845 William McKenzie King sold the land to George K. Chisholm. In the same year George sold it to his brother R. K. Chisholm. It is possible that R. K. Chisholm had a commercial building erected on the land in 1852, for in that year he took out a mortgage for $400 with the Bank of Upper Canada. In 1883 a disastrous fire swept through the business district, levelling whatever might have been standing on this site as well as the impressive four-storey Romain Block to the west. It seems that the lot then stood vacant for the next four years.

Further to the east, on Lakeshore Road at the south east corner of Dunn Street, stood one of Oakville's early hostelries. William O'Reilly purchased the lot from William Chisholm in March of 1840 and promptly took out a mortgage to build a tavern. William O'Reilly operated the business for almost fifteen years and when he died the tavern was turned over to Thomas Lloyd. During Lloyd's tenure as proprietor, it became a wild and unruly place even for those times. John A. Williams, who lived beside the tavern, noted in his reminiscences that the hotel drew a crowd of "whiskey suckers and loafers — a regular zoo." George Baker, a livery operator and Oakville's first constable, took over the operation of the hotel in 1869. He not only launched a program to clean up the clientele but he also remodelled the structure considerably, permitting him to boast accommodation second to none when he

opened his White Oak Hotel in the spring of 1870 with a grand ball. Baker continued to operate the hotel until 1876, when he traded the White Oak with James Young and took over the old Post Inn at Trafalgar Road and Highway No. 5. In 1878 James Young rented a portion of the building to the Grangers, a farmer's co-operative which, in addition to operating a warehouse, attempted to establish a retail grocery business there. James Young later sold the White Oak to one of the Walsh brothers who in 1887 sold the property to the Presbyterian Congregation whose members were anxious to build a new church.

The rough-cast White Oak Hotel was cut into three sections and carted off in three different directions. John A. Williams noted that one section was carried across the street where it was to become 265-267 Lakeshore Road East; another section was moved to the foot of Allan Street at King Street where it was enlarged and faced with brick to serve as a residence; while the third portion was moved west to become number 152 Lakeshore Road East. This lot had been sold in 1887 to Elizabeth Ann Oliphant by R. K. Chisholm for $575.

Elizabeth was the wife of Duncan Oliphant, a farmer turned hotel-keeper, but it is not known if Oliphant used his newly acquired structure as a tavern or rented it as a shop. Elizabeth Oliphant left the property to her daughter Jane and her husband Edmund Gulledge. During the 1920s the building was the home of Allan Gulledge and his wife, Isabella, and it remained their residence until Evelyn Flaherty purchased it in 1945. Evelyn and her husband, Jeffrey Flaherty, lived in

the building for several years until the green shuttered windows were removed and a larger window installed when Flaherty opened his barber shop in 1947.

Although greatly altered on the street level, the upper portion of the hotel remains very much in its original form. Simple corner boards and eave returns define the stucco gable end with the most notable feature being a half-circle fanlight. The window sash of the second storey appears to be a product of the time of the building's move, while the exterior wall treatment of the street level is a contemporary substitute for the "Vitrolite" of the 1940s which it replaces.

Very few know the building as O'Reilly's Tavern or even as the White Oak Hotel, just as few of the next generation will know the building as Flaherty's Barbershop. It is hoped the structure will survive under one name or another as one of the few examples of a style of commercial architecture once common on both sides of the main street.

Circa 1840
St. Andrew's Church

47 REYNOLDS STREET

Until 1836 those adherents of the Catholic faith who lived in the pioneer community of Oakville had no opportunity for worship other than by journeying out into the township and attending one of the Catholic Missions. In that year, a mission was established in Oakville by Father W. P. McDonough, a man who had a great affinity for the Irish immigrants that comprised a sizeable portion of the town's populace.

William Chisholm gave the mission a plot of land at the corner of King and Reynolds Streets, and between 1838 and 1840, under the guidance of Father Eugene O'Reilly, funds were raised by subscription for the erection of the first Catholic Church in Oakville. John Cavan, a carpenter, is recorded as being one of those who generously gave their talents. In addition to such other Catholic families as the Sweeneys, Rigneys, O'Shaughnessys, Boylans, O'Boyles, and McDermotts, it is suggested that the Presbyterians also contributed to the building of the Church.

The three-thousand dollar, clapboard structure measured 37'6" wide by 70' long and was capable of seating two hundred persons when Father O'Reilly said the first mass in October of 1840. The structure, built upon hand-adzed pine beams, some measuring sixty feet in length, sat on a mortarless stone foundation. Pine tree stumps, remnants of the newly cleared land, remain under the floorboards to this day.

Numerous priests attended St. Andrew's over the ensuing years, but because the territory that the priests were expected to cover was so vast, services were held only one week in five. Consequently the more devoted and the more hardy members of the congregation braved a forty-mile return walk to Dundas in order to attend mass on a regular basis.

A burial ground was established on lands to the north of the church, as was the first Presbytery. This one-storey brick cottage was completed in 1858 and Father Fitzgerald was the first resident priest. In 1859 the Oakville Mission came under the charge of Reverend Jeremiah Ryan whose efforts over the next seventeen years caused St. Andrew's to grow enormously. Ryan established St. Mary's Separate School to the east of the church in 1860. This two-storey, twenty-four by thirty-six foot frame building provided classrooms for the 107 children who enrolled the first year. Not all the children who attended the school were of the Catholic faith, and neither were all the children who gathered at the Convent on the south-west corner of Reynolds and King Streets, the new home of the Sisters of St. Joseph, who not only taught school but also gave instruction in music, drawing, and sewing. The Tax Collector, George Sumner, had just cause to record in his diary that "Council met tonight, passed a resolution to let the Catholics collect their own taxes and I am glad of it." In 1870 the nave of the church was extended to permit the seating of 300 persons, and it was then that the exterior was most likely given a roughcast stucco finish. Carpenter and joiner James Connor Sr. created three ornate altars, and these were in all likelihood installed at the new east end of the church at that time.

In 1880, George Sumner recorded in his diary, "I was at the funeral of the Rev. J. Ryan, Catholic Priest—there were 18 Priests in the church." With the passing away of the much-respected Ryan, various other priests assumed the leadership of St. Andrew's. However, one very popular tradition persisted. George Sumner noted in July of 1898: "I was down to Father Burkes Garden Party." And again in July, 1900: "The Catholic Garden Party tonight and they always draw a big crowd."

In 1916 the old church was thoroughly renovated and the new chancel was added at that time. A donation of a large electric chandelier from Mr. W. S. Davis, a prominent businessman and supporter of the English Church, was made during this period of renovation.

Today St. Andrew's Church is a handsome white structure presenting much the same appearance as it did when it was built. The corners of the building are emphasized by stucco-covered, chamfered quoins, and the pediment of the gable end is dramatized by a steeple that, according to the *County of Halton Directory* of 1870, rises 150 feet in the air. The octagonal spire, sheathed in slate shingles, is set upon an octagonal louvred loft over a short tower. A deep, boldly trimmed frieze, approximately two feet in height, forms a broad ribbon under the cornice. Apart from the small stained glass windows near the chancel, each of the long sides of the nave are illuminated by four large, tinted, pointed-arch windows. Two similar windows flank the main entry. The glazing bars in the head of these windows display a simple interlacing design. The interior window sash is wide and delicately moulded. Plaster cornices, painted borders, and three central medallions festoon the ceiling. The sixteen-foot deep loft, reached by a staircase that passes across the northerly front window, houses the organ.

St. Andrew's is the only religious building to survive intact the early beginnings of the town. Like the Methodist Church, built at the same time, St. Andrew's classic design and pleasing proportions bear a striking similarity to many Neo-Classic churches erected in Britain and the eastern United States during the eighteenth and early nineteenth centuries.

Circa 1844
The Joshua Leach House

1493 LAKESHORE ROAD EAST

Tucked in behind a stone wall in a stand of trees, the settled appearance of this Georgian-style cottage belies the truth, for it was moved to this site in 1922 and set upon the foundations of an earlier building.

Born in the United States in 1776, Joshua Leach arrived in the town of York at the age of twenty-one to ply his trade of carpentry. There his work gained the attention of government officials, and in addition to general carpentry jobs he was commissioned, among other things, to fashion a chair for the Legislative Council. For this he received the handsome sum of £ 7. Lieutenant-Governor Francis Gore paid Leach £ 25 for the pulpit he created for St. James, the first church in York. The growing town provided much work for this talented man and enough financial return for him to purchase, in 1822, a 200-acre parcel of land some two miles east of what was to become the town of Oakville.

Here Leach and his American-born wife, Mary, built a home for their family that eventually numbered eight children. Within a few years he established a saw-mill and shortly thereafter a thrashing-mill on what is now known as Joshua Creek. As the mills flourished, so did his reputation as a creator of fine millwork and delicate carpentry. In addition to supplying the sash for the Temperance Hall and many of the other buildings in the new town, Joshua taught three of his sons Robert, Ransom, and William his skills so that they too would leave their marks as fine carpenters and builders.

In 1834, Joshua bought from King's College thirty-six acres south of the Lake Shore Road, and six years later he sold twenty of these to his son William. In 1844, Joshua, who was by then sixty-eight years of age, turned the operation of the mill at the top of Still's Lane over to his son William. Joshua and Mary moved into the small home he had built for their retirement on the sixteen acres he retained. Joshua's new home displays the sense of classic proportion and fine detail he knew as a cabinet maker and reflects the appreciation the man had for architectural scale and symmetry. The five-bay front with its

central hall illuminated by sidelights and fanlight, the reverse staircase (a vestige of earlier times), and the six-panel doors are all in the spirit of the true Georgian. The exterior, with its boldly moulded cornice and imaginative returns, like the interior wainscoting and chair rails, commanded the hands of a master woodworker.

Joshua Leach died at the age of eighty-six and shortly thereafter his wife and son Charles sold the house. A long list of owners held the property over the ensuing years. In 1910 Mr. James Ryrie bought the house as an investment. Twelve years later it was moved to its present location to serve as a staff building to house the orchard manager of Mr. Harry Ryrie.

The house later changed hands many times, finally to be abandoned and slated for demolition. The building was saved from this fate by new owners who restored it to its present condition. Originally this one-and-a-half storey timber-framed house consisted of a principal room on either side of the hall and a small secondary room behind each, with two bedrooms upstairs. The new tail, sympathetic in design to the original building, replaces one that had been added shortly after the move. A wider front porch was left behind. However, the present porch, added after the house was set in its new location, is entirely compatible with the detail of the façade. Joshua Leach would be pleased.

Circa 1847
The William Cantley House

126 BATH STREET

The land this house stands on was once part of a holding described as park lots A and B. These lots ran north from the lake to Bath Street and stretched from Kerr Street west to St. Jude's Cemetery. It has been suggested that the Reverend Robert Murray and his wife occupied a house at the foot of Bath Street and that as early as 1837 it had served as a rectory for Matthew Lyon. Murray ministered to the Presbyterians in Oakville and the surrounding countryside until he accepted the position of Superintendent of Education for Canada West in Kingston in the year 1842. It would seem that the Murray house was of an earlier vintage than the house presently on the site.

In March of 1847 William Cantley, a retired bank director, purchased park lots A and B from an investment company and proceeded to erect a one-storey brick house that summer. In July of that year the Presbyterian records disclose that Cantley, a yeoman or landowner, his wife, and Daniel Owens, a servant man, were admitted to the Presbyterian Congregation. Cantley, born in 1791 in the parish of New Deer, Aberdeenshire, Scotland, and his wife Christian Ord, born in 1790 in the parish of Pitsligo, were both in their late fifties when he purchased the land. The Census of 1851 befittingly describes William Cantley as a gentleman and their home as a one-storey brick structure. Ten years later the Census reported that the structure was still one-storey in height. Cantley had by this time disjoined the Presbyterian Congregation to become a member of the English Church. On his twelve-acre holding, William Cantley, the gentleman farmer, had ample time to assist the Oakville Grammar School in the capacity of trustee.

In March of 1872 Cantley's wife Christian died at the age of eighty-two. Within four months, the eighty-one-year-old William remarried, as the Presbyterian records note that "Mrs. Mary Cantley of Oakville joined July 7, 1872 from East Kinloss." William rejoined the Presbyterian Church at that time as well, and the same record notes that he passed away three years later.

The Collector's Rolls report that Mrs. Mary Cantley, now twice widowed, was owner of the property in 1877. Two years later she married James Johnston, a medical doctor, at her home on Bath Street. The marriage was performed by the Reverend Mr. Worrell and witnessed by N. J. Wellwood, principal of the high school. In 1905 Mary Johnston sold the property for $6,600 to Percy A. Bath. Formerly of Montreal and Toronto, Bath was an accountant and official with the Toronto brokerage house of Pellatt and Pellatt.

Percy and Ruth Bath raised their four children in their new home they called "Belair Farm." On the rolling land to the west Bath erected a series of poultry houses where he raised chickens and pigeons. The booklet *Oakville* published in 1912 stated that "very few in Canada have entered this business, but now at Oakville, Mr. P. A. Bath has established a pigeon farm and is breeding thousands of Garneaux pigeons, a Belgian bird of large size, the young of which are reputed as the finest known squab." A two-storey barn standing closer to the house served as a storage shed for the "Belair Jam Factory," an operation Bath established to market the great quantity of fruit produced on his farm. Bath was also a partner with Mr. V. Robin in the Oakville Garage. This "first-class, up-to-date garage" held the exclusive agency for the Reo Special and the "famous Ford machine" in the Oakville district and stocked a full line of Ford parts.

Percy Bath was an original member of St. Jude's Advisory Board, auditor of the Trafalgar Agricultural Society and president of the Boy Scout Council. He was elected first president of the Oakville Club and was highly regarded as a yachtsman. In 1919 he was appointed Clerk Treasurer of the Town of Oakville and "the town was fortunate in being able to secure the services of a man with the outstanding qualifications of Mr. Bath."

In 1923 Bath purchased blocks 100, 101, 76, and almost all of block 71, extending his land holding up to Lakeshore Road. Several years after the death in 1928 of Ruth Bath, the ownership of Belair once again changed hands; this time to her daughter Margaret (Twitto) Wilson and her husband Franklin. The Wilsons had previously lived in a small cottage across the street at 111 Bath Street. The Wilsons sold the property in 1949 and it remained in the possession of Mr. and Mrs. Wilder Breckenridge until 1972. In 1967 the

Town of Oakville changed the name of that section of Anderson Street west of the reservoir to Bath Street in honour of Percy Bath.

The William Cantley House is similar to "Holyrood," the nearby Anglican Rectory. Erected in 1853, it too was built of brick in one-storey and later enlarged by a second storey. Originally the Cantley House fronted on the lake and was approached by a circular drive that extended from the end of Walker Street. A large verandah, designed to protect the front-entry, stretches the breadth of the structure, providing a splendid place from which to view the expansive grounds that run down to the lake. A central hall extends through the structure from front to back where an identical doorway on the north side serves as the present front door.

Both doors bear original box locks and each door is composed of six panels. They are surrounded by an identical architrave, sidelights, and transom light. The panels of the exterior doors are recessed on the outside, but the panel shape is merely incised into the wood surface on the interior. The remaining doors in the house are of six-panel construction and are all enclosed by broad, deeply moulded door surrounds. The gracious interior is enhanced with a ceiling height of 10'2". The baseboards measure a generous fifteen inches in depth, and an equally expansive wood trim is displayed in the panels beneath the windows and on the angular window recesses. The windows are broad and high and the opening is composed of

six-over-six lights, each measuring 12" × 18". The fireplaces on the second storey have been closed over, but three fireplaces remain on the main floor of the house. The two in the principal rooms are of a simple, classic design, while the fireplace in the lesser room is smaller and contains an iron fire-box and grate.

A small one-storey wing to the west appears to have been a later addition, and although it rests on several hand-adzed beams, many of the joists are of a later vintage than the 2¾" × 12½" joists of the main part of the house. The addition seems to have been constructed of salvaged materials and created to serve initially as a kitchen or as staff quarters. It is uncertain when the second storey was added; however, the broad hall comfortably accommodates the beautifully crafted flying staircase that leads to the upper level. The imaginative design and the finely tapered balusters are the work of skilled and discerning joiners.

The addition of the second storey is not obvious on the brickwork because the exterior

has been treated with a wash of paint. A. J. Downing, an American advocate of good architectural design and a man of discriminating taste, describes this "brick wash" in his book *The Architecture of Country Houses* published in 1850:

"Cheap wash for cottages of Brick, stone, stucco or rough-cast. Take a barrel, and slake half a bushel of fresh lime as before mentioned; then fill the barrel two-thirds full of water and add 1 bushel of hydraulic cement or water lime. Dissolve in water and add 3 lbs. sulphate of zinc. The whole should be of the thickness of paint, ready for use with the brush. This wash is improved by the addition of a peck of white sand and stirred in just before using it. The color is a pale stone-color, nearly white. To make it fawn color, add 1 lb. yellow ochre, 2 lbs. raw umber, 2 lbs. Indian red. To make it drab, add 1 lb. Indian red, 1 lb. umber, 1 lb. lampblack."

White mortar strips were drawn over the wash further to disguise the wall extension at the same time. The brick quoins and the lintels over the door openings were also treated with a light-coloured wash to simulate either stonework or a polychrome brick pattern. All in all, the William Cantley House is a stately brick home that imparts every impression of having been designed as a two-storey structure. It retains the character that has been shaped by the former owners, a retired banker and a retired accountant, both gentleman farmers.

Circa 1848
The George K. Chisholm House

85 NAVY STREET

In 1840, at age twenty-six, George King Chisholm, son of the founder of Oakville, married Isabella Land, grand-daughter of the founder of Hamilton. The couple lived in Hamilton for several years before they moved to Oakville around 1847. In 1848 George purchased, from the Gore Bank, a lot at the corner of Navy and Robinson Streets, and there he had erected a one-and-a-half storey brick house. It was one of four brick houses in the town at the time.

George and Isabella had eight children of whom only five survived childhood. Like his father William, George Chisholm became deeply involved in both municipal and provincial affairs. In 1847 Chisholm was Chairman of the Board of Health. In 1852 he was President of the Mechanic's Institute and of the Oakville Agricultural Society. He was Chairman of the Board of Education, Worshipful Master of the White Oak Lodge, Lieutenant Colonel of the 1st Battalion of Halton Volunteers and Serjeant-at-Arms in the Parliament. Chisholm was Town Reeve for three years, Councillor for fourteen years, and Mayor of Oakville for eight years.

Chisholm joined his brother John A. Chisholm in the operation of a grist mill in 1853. In 1857 he sold his house in town and moved to a new, more impressive home he had built on his 260-acre farm on the west side of the river.

Dr. Edwy J. Ogden, who gave his place of residence as "of Oakville and Chicago," and his wife Mary purchased the home for £530 and retained it until 1868. It is not known if he ever dwelt in the house as he owned many properties in town. Ogden sold to Isabella and Richard Shaw Wood. Wood was a native of Bermuda who had come to Oakville during the 1850s. As an entrepreneur he was quick to capitalize on the discovery of oil in Petrolia and founded the Oakville Oil Refinery. His refinery on the east bank of the Sixteen soon became one of the largest suppliers of "coal-oil" in the Canadas, and the purchase of a "gentleman's house" at Navy and Robinson was only befitting his position. Richard Shaw Wood built a two-storey brick addition to the rear of the structure. Although it was supposedly intended for use as a bank, there are no records of it serving that purpose. Edwy J. Ogden's name reappears in 1875 when he remarried. His second wife was Sarah Shaw Wood, the daughter of Richard and Isabella.

Richard Shaw Wood owned a planing mill and blind factory during the 1870s and he was successful with this endeavour as he was with his oil refinery. The following newspaper quotation from 1878 bears this out: "Messrs R. S. Wood & Co. carried off first prizes for sashes, doors, mouldings and blinds at the County Show last week." In the same year, Richard Shaw Wood sold the house for $1,300 to Mary Ann and Thomas Patterson.

Both Mary Ann and Thomas were highly respected and each had gained wide-spread reputations. He as a custom tailor of gentlemen's clothing and she as a milliner of fine ladies' hats and bonnets. Thomas Patterson, like the original owner of the house, responding to the call of civic duty, acted as a Justice of the Peace and in 1894 served a term as Mayor of Oakville. In 1903 the Pattersons sold the house and another lot to Captain Maurice Fitzgerald for $1,900.

At age fifteen, Fitzgerald had signed up on the schooner *Junius* and begun his career on the Lakes. Within ten years he received his master's papers and his first command. Fitzgerald, refusing to captain a steamship as the last of the sailing schooners disappeared from the lakes, returned instead to the land and entered the coal-and-lumber business. Captain Fitzgerald, who died in 1931 at eighty-seven years of age, lived at 85 Navy Street for over twenty years.

A flat, pitched roof holds the storey-and-a-half G. K. Chisholm house securely to the

ground, while a tall, split double chimney springs out from the north wall. The chimney, supported by decorative arches, projects over and above the porch roof. The porch, with its impressive treillage, surrounds the house on three sides and overshadows the entry.

The front door is of a four-panel design with an incised groove down the centre to simulate double doors. Bright scarlet sidelights, etched in a floral design, complete the simple doorcase. The intricate trellis work contains broad elliptical arches yet displays a Chinese influence in the composition of straight wooden bars. The side walls of the house contain French-style casement windows of sixteen lights to the pair, while the fenestration of the front façade comprises glazed doors, floor to ceiling, of twenty lights to the pair.

The George K. Chisholm House is a fine example of the Regency style. Although not a colonist, Chisholm was a gentleman, an officer, and a politician, and his ideals were very much those of his contemporaries who immigrated to this new land. Successive owners must surely have been stirred by the architectural innovations of the G. K. Chisholm House, for at one time it acquired the romantic name "Glen Prossen."

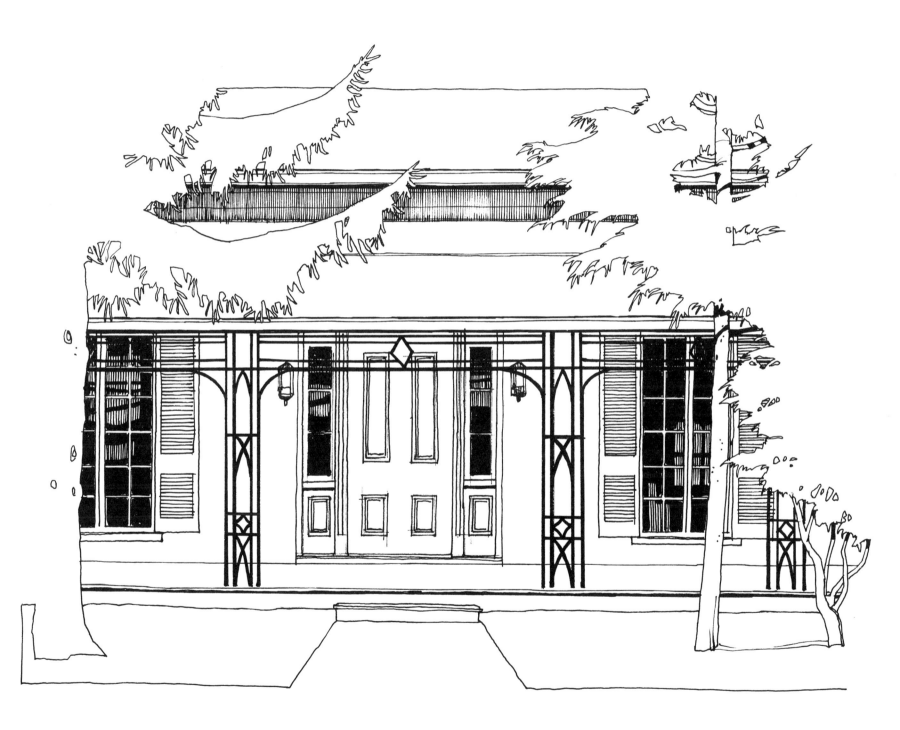

Circa 1852
The James Connor House

75 REYNOLDS STREET

Born in 1814 in Wexford in the south of Ireland, James Connor arrived in Oakville before the middle of the nineteenth century. He and his wife Catherine had seven children and of the four boys, two, James Jr. and William, took up their father's trade, becoming carpenters. According to the Assessment Rolls of 1852, James Connor was renting a building at the corner of George and Church Streets. In that year he purchased the lot at the corner of Reynolds and Robinson Streets, and there he built the house that presently stands on the lot. The building at George and Church Streets could have been either a dwelling or a carpentry shop.

James Connor was both a carpenter and joiner. In addition to building many houses in town, he was responsible for creating a curved altar rail for his church. Unfortunately the rail has disappeared over the course of numerous additions to the interior of St. Andrew's. Similarly, many of the houses that contained the hanging staircases, for which Connor was renowned, have also disappeared.

James Connor Sr. was in partnership with one or more of his sons according to a newspaper advertisement of June 1873. "New Blind, Sash & Door Factory. (Under Hagaman's Carriage Factory). Mouldings of every description on hand and to order. Connor & Co. proprietors." The *Express and County of Halton Advertiser* of July 1877 displayed the following announcement regarding another house in the neighbourhood: "For sale or to let. That beautiful new and commodious family residence situated near the R.C. Church commanding a magnificent view of Lake Ontario, contains nine rooms and two halls. Is quite new. Terms reasonable. Apply to Mr. Bailey, *Express* Office or to Mr. James Connors, Snr., the builder." Although he signed his name to legal documents as "Connor" and he had many times been recorded as "Conner" or "Conners," the family has become known as "O'Connor." In 1894, the year he died, the eighty-year-old Connor was still recorded as a carpenter. The James Connor House stayed in the hands of the family for many years after his death, and it was only in the 1960s that it was purchased and restored to its present condition.

The Connor House is a well-proportioned, one-and-a-half storey clapboard cottage with a three-bay front and central hall. The sharply projecting cornice and broad frieze of this simple house are dramatized by knife-edged eave returns. Delicate capitals top the corner-board pilasters. The porch railing has been rebuilt, and although the original four-panel front door has been replaced by a new six-panel door, the door architrave has survived admirably. A geometric arrangement of wooden glazing bars creates a striking pattern in a deep transom light. The transom bar, elaborately treated with a repeating lozenge design, is supported by a broad scroll-shaped bracket on each of the two flat pilasters. The window sash is composed of two lights, each of six panes. Inside, all windows on the front portion of the structure are embellished by deeply chamfered panels below the sills.

The room immediately behind the front parlour, which has a wainscoting of broad horizontal planks, may have been the original kitchen, while the wainscoting in the present kitchen in the tail is of the vertical tongue-

and-groove variety. Unlike the exquisite staircases he crafted for others, a space-saving enclosed staircase in the centre of the house leads up to what was once one large room. His grandson Charles McDermott recalls seeing Connor's workbench laden with moulding planes and other hand tools in this upper room. It was divided into four bedrooms after the turn of the century, when the house was occupied by Connor's daughters Catherine and Maria, and later Maria's daughter Mary Markey, her husband, and their children. James Connor Sr. was obviously a craftsman, and it is apparent that he took great pride in his modest home, for it has been embellished with many fine details and the elaborate woodwork one would expect to find in a much larger house.

Circa 1853
The Reverend George Washington House

417 LAKESHORE ROAD WEST

The Reverend George Washington was born in Ireland in 1800 and in the 1840s he and his wife Susan came to Canada. Washington, a Wesleyan Methodist, served as a circuit rider until 1853 when he retired from this rigorous position to take up farming. In that year he purchased a portion of the William McCraney farm. He had a brick, one-storey Regency cottage erected on a rise of land just north of the Lake Shore Road facing onto a small brook. The Reverend Mr. Washington named his home "Retreat."

The Washingtons had four daughters; however, only two, Susan and Georgina, lived to adulthood. Alicia died at the age of ten and Farina, who was born in the house, died when she was nineteen in an asylum. The Washingtons lived in the "Retreat" for twenty years, and in 1874 they sold the cottage and nine acres to Hugh Francis Pullen, who had just arrived from England. At age forty-nine, Pullen was a widower. His eight-year-old daughter, Hester, had recently died and he had just retired from the Royal Navy as Paymaster in Chief. British law forbade him to marry the sister of his deceased wife, Mary Ann, who had been caring for his children. Consequently he emigrated to Canada and two months later, when Ellen Skinley and his four remaining children arrived at Lévis, Quebec, they were immediately married.

Hugh, Ellen, and the four children, Hugh Garnett, Alfred, Charles, and Emily, moved into the "Retreat" which Pullen renamed "Clifton" in memory of the family home "Cliff House" in England. Three children, Ellen, Frank, and Ernest, were born to the Pullens in "Clifton," and in 1878 Pullen's unmarried sister from England joined them there. Hugh Pullen added a second storey in the form of a mansard roof in order to accommodate his growing family. After nine years the damp lake air had aggravated Pullen's respiratory condition, forcing him

to sell the house and move to Brantford in January of 1883. Hugh F. Pullen died in September of that year. Three years later, his wife Ellen moved to Toronto and later returned to Oakville where her sons Frank and Ernest subsequently established families.

Thomas Walsh who purchased the house from Pullen was both carpenter and hotel-keeper by trade and operated various establishments over the years. John A. Williams recorded in his diary that Walsh "had a large family and not being a great worker—family had only enough to eat—but scrupulously clean. He lived near lake and kept a scow for gathering driftwood." The Walshes renamed the house "Rosedale Villa" and Mrs. Walsh took in boarders to supplement their income. "Rosedale Villa" soon became one of the most popular guest houses in Oakville, and every summer it was filled to capacity with repeat visitors from Toronto and Hamilton as well as such places as Kingston and Collingwood and far-away centres as Edmonton and New York.

In 1900 the property was purchased by Captain George Morden. Born in 1837, Morden served on both schooners and steamers and eventually developed his own shipping line to transport lumber from the Georgian Bay district. Morden invested heavily in land and amassed over a thousand acres by the time he died in 1908. It is probable that the Reverend George Washington's House was just another investment and that he never lived in it. The property remained with the Morden family, and various members did live in the house until 1943 when it was purchased by Mr. and Mrs. Alexander Downey. Other than the addition of three more dormer windows and the enlargement of the cellar, the only major change implemented by the Downeys was to replaster the entire interior of the house. Originally plaster had been applied directly to the brick walls of the first floor. This and the plaster work of the second

storey were stripped away to permit the addition of insulation. Alexander Downey started raising gladioli as a hobby, but by 1953, the year he died, the several patches of flowers had grown to several acres of gladioli and a thriving business.

In 1975 the cottage was sold to Josef and Norma Petriska, and after one hundred years the old barn at the rear of the property, built under the direction of Hugh Pullen, was converted by Petriska into a sculpture studio. The building the Downeys used to dry gladioli bulbs serves as exhibit space for local art groups.

Originally the Reverend George Washington House displayed all the typical Regency characteristics. It is most fortunate that the French doors on the front and rear, the protective verandahs, and the broad doorcase with sidelights and transom light were not adversely affected when the mansard roof, so popular in the last half of the Victorian era, replaced the Regency cottage roof. The wide central hall permitted Pullen to install a handsome staircase which was stripped of layers of dark and chequered varnish by the Downeys. Four panel doors and generous foot-high baseboards are common throughout the house. Originally two parlours separated by a broad arch graced the southerly half of the structure. The archway has been reduced and the rear parlour turned into a kitchen to service the front parlour which is now a dining room. The living room is presently a large room on the north side of the house.

When Downey enclosed the verandah on the east side, he used wood cut from his own woodlot which he had milled at a local sawmill, just as Washington or Pullen would have done. Downey obviously had great affection for the "Retreat," "Clifton," or "Rosedale Villa," as it was variously named, just as the present owners do.

Circa 1854
The Peter MacDougald House

29 THOMAS STREET

Contrary to its appearance this impressive, well-proportioned home was built in three stages over a period of nearly ninety years. Although it appears to be a wing off the main structure the original section, the lower block with a gently sloping roof was built in 1839. Set over a lake-stone cellar and constructed of heavy timber framing, this 20′ × 25′ dwelling was first sheathed in clapboard and very likely was lathed and plastered when Peter MacDougald purchased the property and increased the size of the structure considerably.

Peter Archibald MacDougald was born in 1823 of Scottish immigrants. Peter grew up in the Talbot Settlement in the western district of Upper Canada and came to Oakville as a young man in 1844. Here he found employment with Alexander Proudfoot, one of the first merchants to set up shop in Trafalgar Township. MacDougald worked with Proudfoot for four years, from whom, in addition to shop-keeping, he learned the art of buying, selling, and shipping timber, staves, potash, and a variety of farm produce, the principal item being wheat. After a stint of several years spent in the Georgetown area, he returned to Oakville in 1854 where he was offered a partnership with William Romain in a grain-buying business. It seems that MacDougald and Romain operated the grain warehouse on the banks of the Sixteen at the foot of Robinson Street shortly thereafter. In 1854 in preparation for his upcoming marriage to Mary Jane Chisholm, daughter of William Chisholm, MacDougald purchased two lots on Thomas Street and the original house. The thirty-one year old MacDougald had achieved considerable success by this time, and accordingly he chose to remodel the old house to suit his lifestyle and assumed a large mortgage of £2,500. According to the Collector's Rolls of 1867, MacDougald's house was assessed at two-and-one-half times the 1853 value when John Rivel lived there.

As illustrated in the plans, MacDougald enlarged the original structure with a 62′ × 20′ addition. This one-storey shed with a lean-to roof was erected across the rear forming the letter "T" shape. The northerly portion with wide barn doors was used as a stores room for MacDougald's brokerage business, and the adjoining room served as a small office so that he might conduct transactions from within his home. A kitchen and dining room constituted that area directly behind the original block, and two bedrooms were placed in the southerly section and three on the second storey. The second-storey windows are composed of a six-over-six pane configuration and are of such ample proportions that the sills sit just above the floor level. Although the shed-roofed addition appears to have been of a most utilitarian nature, MacDougald bestowed on the original block such refinements of the time as six sets of double French doors of a most distinctive construction, set in ten-inch-wide architraves, and a fashionable verandah embroidered with treillage on three sides. The whole was given a coat of stucco the better to unite the two blocks and conform to the Regency pattern.

Peter and Mary were married in May of 1855 by the Reverend James Nisbet in the old Presbyterian Church, and they raised three children in the home that MacDougald called "Glenorchy." According to carpenter James McDonald's records, considerable work was done on the property in 1869. In that year, McDonald added such improvements as the wooden fence that once ran the length of the block and a privy for which he charged $6.50. McDonald also records work on the stable during that period. Built with hand-adzed beams of a timber-frame construction and broad planks, as much as fifteen inches wide, this stable with a loft overhead gave room to a carriage and horse in the one-box stall. The semi-elliptical arch over the double doors, characteristic of the Neo-Classic era, suggests

that it could date from the time of the original structure.

P. A. MacDougald was one of the first councillors when the Town of Oakville became incorporated in 1857, and in 1875 he was elected Mayor and remained in office for nine years. During that time the Citizen's Band gave concerts on many occasions on the lawns of Glenorchy to which the townspeople were invited. A business directory of 1865-66 lists MacDougald as a grain and produce merchant and he is recorded similarly in 1874-75. In addition to retailing everyday grocery items, MacDougald was also one of the principal fleece brokers in the area. In 1883 a disastrous fire wiped out much of the business section, including MacDougald's store in the Romain Block. After this incident MacDougald is recorded as having difficulties maintaining control in Council meetings, and in April of the following year he disappeared for several days. George Sumner noted a week later, on April 24, 1884: "P. A. MacDougald died this morning at 5 o'clock of congestion of the liver caused by exposure & whiskey." Some time later the property came into the hands of William Joyce. Joyce came to town during the 1870s and the *Ontario Gazeteer and Directory* of 1887 listed him, like MacDougald, as the proprietor of a general store.

The building aged over the ensuing years. When Mr. A. Montye Macrae purchased the property in 1926, it, like the surrounding neighbourhood, was in great need of attention. Macrae enlisted the Toronto architectural firm of George, Moorhouse and King and principally the services of his neighbour Colonel Walter Moorhouse who lived in the old George Sumner House. Moorhouse was most sympathetic to the structure and drew up the plans reproduced herein.

The surrounding verandah was removed as were the entry and the interior staircase of the old block. The entire ground floor space was given over to a most commodious parlour now filled with sunlight. The verandah posts were recycled to form a grape arbour and a new porch was erected to shelter the main entrance. The lower walls of the lean-to structure were retained and extended upward to create a gabled structure of two-and-one-half storeys. The dining room was enlarged and pushed to the south in order to make room for a new, broad central staircase. MacDougald's stores room was converted to servant's quarters, and the office became a "sitting room" for the new owner who, as a keen yachtsman, had the room outfitted with white panelling and trimmed with mahogany moulding. Moorhouse was also responsible for the interesting addition of a small round window, high on the western gable, bearing the dates 1839 and 1927.

Almost fifty years passed before the house again changed hands. The new owners have commenced a faithful restoration program.

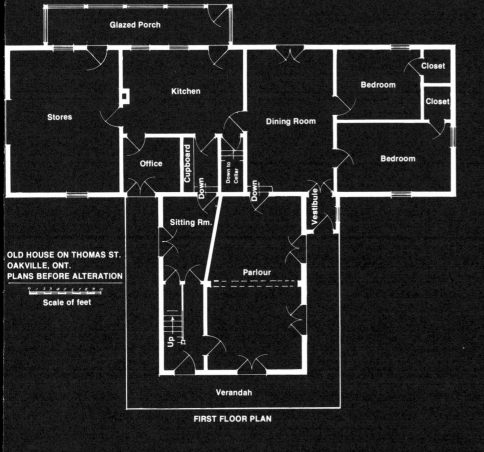

Glazed Porch

Stores

Kitchen

Office

Cupboard

Dining Room

Bedroom

Closet

Closet

Bedroom

Down

Down to Cellar

Down

Vestibule

Sitting Rm.

Parlour

Up

Verandah

**OLD HOUSE ON THOMAS ST.
OAKVILLE, ONT.
PLANS BEFORE ALTERATION**

0 1 2 3 4 5 6 7 8 9
Scale of feet

FIRST FLOOR PLAN

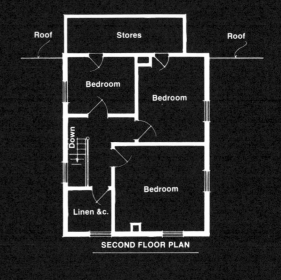

Roof

Stores

Roof

Bedroom

Bedroom

Down

Bedroom

Linen &c.

SECOND FLOOR PLAN

**ALTERATIONS TO HOUSE ON THOMAS ST., OAKVILLE
FOR A. MONTYE MACRAE, ESQ.**
Scale: ½ inch = one foot

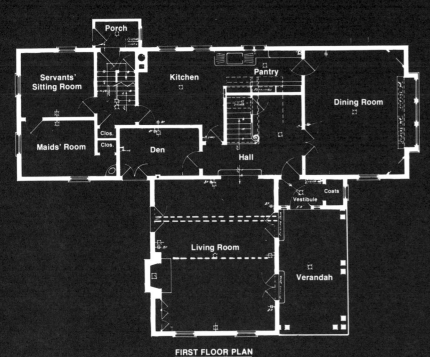

Porch

**Servants'
Sitting Room**

Kitchen

Pantry

Dining Room

Maids' Room

Clos.

Clos.

Den

Hall

Coats

Vestibule

Living Room

Verandah

FIRST FLOOR PLAN

**ALTERATIONS TO HOUSE ON THOMAS ST., OAKVILLE,
FOR A. MONTYNE MACRAE, ESQ.**
Scale: ¼ inch = one foot

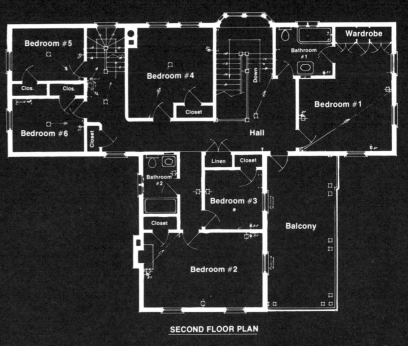

Bedroom #5

Clos.

Clos.

Bedroom #6

Closet

Bedroom #4

Closet

**Bathroom
#1**

Wardrobe

Bedroom #1

Down

Hall

**Bathroom
#2**

Closet

Linen

Closet

Bedroom #3

Balcony

Bedroom #2

SECOND FLOOR PLAN

51

Circa 1855
The Matthew Barclay House

215 WILLIAM STREET

The Barclay House has often been referred to as the Arnott house, and although the two families were related in business and by marriage, no evidence has been uncovered to confirm Arnott ownership.

The Census of 1841 reveals that James Arnott owned land and farmed in Trafalgar Township. It states also that at that time he had been a resident in Canada for eight years and that he shared his residence with his British-born wife, Jane Scotland, and their five children; Jane, Margaret, Anna, David, and Charles, who had all been born in Scotland.

Shortly after the census was taken, Arnott sold his farm and moved his family into Oakville where he set himself up as a general merchant, selling groceries and dry goods. When the Presbyterian Congregation was formed in 1846, James Arnott was one of the original members. In 1855 he was appointed Trustee to the Oakville Grammar School and in that same year, when he was sixty years of age, he moved his business from a shop he rented on the north side of Lakeshore Road between Thomas and George Streets to a new three-storey, brick building on the northeast corner of the block. This was one of a pair of buildings that he shared with John Barclay. *The Great Western Railway Gazeteer and Directory* of 1861-62 ran the following advertisement. "James Arnott, dealer in Dry Goods, groceries, provisions, clothing, hats, caps, crockery etc. Colborne Street. Oakville C.W." During the years Arnott resided in Oakville, the Collector's Rolls make no mention of his owning a dwelling house; however, there are numerous records describing him as a tenant on various properties, and some of these obviously refer to his mercantile operations. In 1867 James Arnott was listed as a tenant in the house owned by Joseph Clark now known as "Rose Cottage." James Arnott died in 1874.

Matthew and Mary Barclay came out from Paisley, Scotland, in 1832 to farm in Trafalgar Township. Like Arnott's, the Presbyterian records of 1846 mention Barclay's name and note that he was an Elder of the Congregation and that he was living in the township with his wife and their ten children in that year. In 1853 the Collector's Rolls list Barclay as a resident in the township, but in February of 1855 Registry Office records note the sale of the property, now 215 William street, to Matthew Barclay by George K. Chisholm. Matthew Barclay was by then seventy-four, consequently it was not surprising to discover that in October of that year, time enough for the house to have been completed, the property was transferred to his sons, John and Matthew, who were the executors of his estate. In that same year John Barclay moved his business into the new brick building adjoining James Arnott's store. As a young man Barclay had assisted in the Post Office that backed on Arnott's old shop, and in 1849 he took a position as clerk with W. F. Romain whereby he learned the dual role of grain buyer and general merchant. In 1853 John Barclay married Arnott's daughter, Jane Scotland Arnott. Matthew and Mary Barclay remained in the house at 215 William Street, and after her husband's death Mary continued to live there. The Collector's Rolls of 1873 record her as owner of the property. Mary died in 1881 and a few years later, in 1886, the executors sold the property to John Barclay's wife Jane for $700.

The plan of the Town of Oakville published in 1863 by Michael Hughes shows that John Barclay was living at 214 William Street. With the purchase of his father's home in 1886, he moved his wife and six children across the street to 215, selling his old house to Stafford Marlatt.

Barclay and Arnott were burned out of their brick buildings in 1868, and Arnott who was then sixty-seven gave up business, but Barclay moved across the street to occupy the corner store of the Romain Block. In addition to his grain purchases, Barclay gained fame as a wool buyer and developed a sizeable trade in dry goods, clothing, and groceries. When the Romain Block was devastated by fire in April of 1883, Barclay acquired the same location in the new premises completed just before Christmas in the same year.

John Barclay assumed his share of civic responsibilities, and between the years 1857 and 1881 he served as Councillor for fifteen years, Reeve for four years, and Mayor for four years. Like his father, he was an Elder in the Presbyterian Church, and like his father-in-law he took an active interest in the school system. Barclay served four terms as chairman of the school board and played a significant role in establishing a high school in Oakville. According to George Sumner's diaries, when Barclay died in the winter of 1900, all the school children, trustees, and councillors marched in a procession to the church.

John Barclay's business was carried on by his son, Robert Burns Barclay, who had previously been in charge of the dry good section. The R. B. Barclay business was one of the longest-established stores in Oakville.

In 1904 the executors of John Barclay's will sold the house for $1,500 to the Merchants Bank of Canada to serve as a residence for senior bank employees. In 1907 Herbert Read as a bank employee brought his family to Oakville and to the Barclay House, and by 1917 he was manager of the Merchants Bank. In 1924 the house was sold to the Bank of Montreal, and in 1936 Herbert Read purchased the property. It remained in the possession of the Read family for over forty years.

The Matthew Barclay house is a substantial frame, two-storey structure with a symmetrical six-bay front and gable end chimneys. The central door was once sheltered by a small flat roofed porch complete with balustrade. All that remains are two flat pilasters that frame the doorway and support a simple cornice. The door surround is composed of fluted columns and a deeply recessed transom light which, like the six-over-six window sash and original shutter blinds, have successfully survived the loss of the porch. Numerous requirements over the years have resulted in a long two-storey tail and an enclosed porch. These additions are covered with a fine clapboard siding while the exterior sheathing of the original structure is of a broad cove siding. Though it is of frame construction like many of its contemporaries, Matthew Barclay's house presents a solid, firmly planted appearance reminiscent of the stone houses of his native Scotland.

Circa 1855
The James Reid Store

145 LAKESHORE ROAD EAST

Between 1846 and 1857 Oakville grew from a village of five hundred to a thriving town of two thousand inhabitants. Businessmen eagerly expanded their interests to match the influx of new residents and to cope with the inevitable day when Oakville would be a city. One such merchant was James Reid.

Born in Scotland in 1817, James Reid arrived in Oakville in 1832 as a youth of fifteen. Both James and Oakville were young and both grew quickly, as he soon got caught up in the mercantile trade of the town. Within ten years he amassed sufficient funds to act as a co-signer for the Oakville Hydraulic Company and, like the others, Reid lost his savings. However, he was obviously well situated for within a short time he purchased Alexander Proudfoot's Oakville store on Lakeshore Road, close by the Oakville House, and in 1846 he added to his acquisitions with the purchase of a storage warehouse on the Sixteen. The original shop was a two-storey frame structure similar to the other buildings that bordered the muddy main street at the time. These shops usually consisted of a six-bay front on the gable end facing the street. This was broken by a verandah that ran the width of the structure. The verandah acted as a covered boardwalk and abutted the verandah and boardwalk of the adjoining buildings.

In 1851 James married Rachel Sumner, daughter of the man who for twenty years operated the Oakville House. The Census of 1851 records that James Reid was a proprietor of a merchant shop and warehouse. It also lists his wife, a son William, age eight, as well as William Sumner Reid, age twenty-three, who was a young brother of Rachel. It is safe to assume that they lived over the shop as that was often the custom. Three children survived Rachel who died at the age of thirty in 1854. Reid was a member of the Church of

England and one of the original Councillors when the town was incorporated. During the fifties, James Reid became one of the most successful grain brokers in Oakville, but as the flow of wheat through the port diminished in the 1860s he began to look elsewhere. Late in the decade he sold the building and moved to the newly formed Province of Manitoba where the promise of new fields of wheat beckoned.

In 1868 William Hixon Young, son of the first proprietor of the Oakville House, purchased the three-storey brick building. William was born at Munn's Corners in 1825. Shortly thereafter his family moved to Oakville; by the age of six, his father had died and his mother was in poor health. William was then placed in the care of various relatives and friends in Oakville. When he was fifteen years of age he became an apprentice to David Duff who taught him the trade of cabinet-maker and the related trades of coffin-maker and undertaker. Upon serving his "full term," W. H. Young was invited in as Duff's partner in the business and here he remained until 1848. At twenty-three he went into business for himself. William Young prospered and twenty years later when Reid vacated the building Young took it over. In addition to producing his own wares, Young became the local agent for Fiske's Metallic Coffins and diversified into a variety of goods. A newspaper advertisement in 1878 announced, "A fresh lot of wall papers in new designs—cheap at W. H. Youngs." Times were lean and Young divided the shop into two, renting out the easterly half to grocer W. G. Hewson in 1879. Young held many civic positions including Police Magistrate, Justice of the Peace, Postmaster, Harbour Master, School Trustee, Councillor, Reeve, and Mayor. In his later years he gave up the undertaking profession and devoted his time to selling insurance and real estate. He left Oakville in 1909 to live in

London where he passed away in his ninety-fifth year.

William Hewson is listed as a clerk in the 1871 Census and as a grocer according to the *Ontario Gazeteer & Directory* of 1887. His son, James took over the shop in 1895 and moved the business in 1907 to premises he had built across the street where he furthered the family reputation as dealers in quality provisions. The James Reid Store has changed hands numerous times and has been known by a variety of names. It has served a multitude of functions, and like its counterparts in other small towns the James Reid Store, under the proprietorship of Mr. Ming, was at one time known as the Savoy Cafe.

Many coats of paint now mask the red brick, and even though the street level shop-face has been drastically altered enough identifiable features remain to serve as reminders of what must have been. Three dormers, once round-headed, but now reshaped for ease of repair, peer over the roof's edge onto the street below like a row of pigeons. Low parapet walls cap the gable side walls to prevent any fire spreading from roof to roof. A bracketed cornice is further supported by a pair of sturdy corner brackets and ornate cornices cap the decoratively eared window sashes of the second storey. A heavy frieze supported by stout capitals at the corners divides the two lower floors of the three-storey edifice.

The James Reid shop on the main street is typical of many that once proudly stood on main streets all across the province. Many have been torn down to make way for more contemporary structures, and an equal number have been destroyed in an attempt to make of them something they are not. Even so, Messrs. Reid, Young, Hewson, and Ming would surely testify to the adaptability of this structure.

Circa 1855
The William Romain House

40 FIRST STREET

William Francis Romain was born in Lower Canada in 1818 and as a young man came up to Brampton where he found employment in the service of a grain merchant. Although this bright young man had become manager of the store in just two years, he was attracted to the flourishing village of Oakville and the prospects of the thriving grain trade there. He established himself in Oakville in 1846 and a year later married Esther Ann, the eldest daughter of William Chisholm. From there his fortunes rose even higher. During the 1850s the flow of grain through the port of Oakville increased steadily, and in 1854 Romain went into partnership with Peter MacDougald. A year later, Peter MacDougald married another of Chisholm's daughters and he became Romain's brother-in-law. In the Census of 1851, W. F. Romain is recorded as a "general merchant, forwarder & agent for life, marine & fire assurance." Later he is recorded as a "dealer in dry goods, groceries, provisions, hardware, etc." In 1853 he was Deputy Reeve, representing Trafalgar Township, and for many years served as Councillor and as Mayor.

By 1855, Oakville was growing at a rapid rate, and with new buildings appearing almost overnight it was decided to expand the village by opening two new surveys, one on

each side of First Street. In that year, Romain bought the strip of land between First and Allan Street, south from the Lakeshore Road to the lake. Romain, whose stature had outgrown the frame dwelling he was listed as living in according to the Census of 1851, contracted for a large brick house to be built on that portion of the land nearest to the lake. Here William and Esther Romain raised six children, and here the children received their schooling. The social standards of early Oakville dictated that the children of certain families, rather than attend the common school, be placed in the charge of a tutor. The Census of 1861 tells us that an Irish governess by the name of Elizabeth Delamore saw to the needs of the Romain children and at the same time taught their cousins, the MacDougald

and Chisholm children. These children, along with those of other affluent families, also attended dance classes in the large dining room. By the mid-1860s the grain tonnage passing through the port was beginning to drop, and in 1869, W. F. Romain filed for bankruptcy, losing the handsome house and all the exquisite furnishings of which he was so proud to his creditors. The *Canadian Champion* of Milton in May 1869 announced a sale of Romain's household effects by auctioneer William Wass. George Sumner wrote in his diary that "Romain's furniture was sold today but T. Chisholm bought it all in." The furnishings were not gone from the family entirely, as Thomas Chisholm was Romain's brother-in-law.

William Romain was one of the outstanding supporters of St. Jude's Church in the early days, but it was not until 1870, when several of his daughters were confirmed, that Romain himself sought confirmation in the Church. After the disastrous loss perhaps it was Romain's acknowledgement of his faith that gave him the will to try again. He reappeared as a general merchant and auctioneer, and although he lived his later years in a fine house, it could never match the grandeur of the house on First Street.

For more than twenty years the Turner family lived on the old Romain estate, and in 1892 it

became the home of the "Gold Cure." In 1904, the Lakehurst Sanitarium advertised an accurate record of ninety-percent permanent cures in the treatment of alcohol, morphine, cocaine, and tobacco addiction. The inmates had full use of the beautiful park-like gardens, the lawn bowling green, tennis courts, and billiard room. "They are at perfect liberty to come and go as they please and under these circumstances a man taking liquor clandestinely would find himself as a traitor to his trust." One wonders what prompted one of the inmates, diamond ring in hand, to inscribe his name on a bedroom window pane.

The Romain House was purchased in 1905 by one of the most successful men the town has ever known. William Sinclair Davis began work in 1879, at age fourteen, delivering telegrams and assisting in the Post Office. By the age of thirty he was established as a real estate agent and over the ensuing years was responsible for attracting hundreds of residents to the County, at the same time handling many of the large estates that grew up in the town. In 1904 William Davis married the young Miss Agnes Cavers, and a year later, when he was forty, they moved into the Romain House. The following year, when they had the first of their five sons, Davis acquired one of the first automobiles in Oakville.

W. S. Davis served as Town Clerk and was elected Mayor of Oakville in 1908. In the same year he entered into a partnership with Charles Doty, forming the Oakville Pressed Brick Works. Located at the foot of the Red Hill, the factory was easily accessible to the clay source. In 1910 Davis was appointed manager of the Bank of Hamilton when it established a branch in Oakville. After the Anderson Bank closed, the Anderson farm was subdivided and Davis was made the exclusive agent for what was known as the Brantwood Survey. Even though the development was premature and very slow to get started, when the Bank of Hamilton merged with the Canadian Bank of Commerce thirteen years later and Davis was given the choice of banker or estate agent, he readily opted for the real estate business. For fifty-one years W. S. Davis was a warden at St. Jude's Church, and it is recorded that his "generosity was only exceeded by his devotion to the temporal affairs of the church." Not only was he generous with his own church, Davis donated a set of large electric lights to St. Andrew's Church.

When Davis purchased the house it was surrounded on three sides by a Regency verandah which he removed and replaced with a small formal portico over the front entrance, a terrace and a sunroom across the rear. During the years the family lived in "Dun-

gannon," as they called the house, it was surrounded by such secondary out-buildings as a stable, capable of accommodating two riding horses and a cow, hen houses, an ice house, a gardener's cottage, and green houses. Other than the stable, these structures are gone, but the fifteen-room house, now divided into apartments, stands as proudly as it did when Romain first lived in it.

It seems that the northern section of the house, which appears to be a wing, was indeed the original structure, and that the larger section to the south was added shortly thereafter. The rooms in the small wing then became servants' quarters. The house would not have been laid out as it is if the wing were a later addition. This Georgian-style residence displays a symmetrical six-bay façade with a central hall. Stone quoins and a stone course between storeys and at the sill contrast with the red brick and add to the appearance of solidarity. Wide overhanging eaves supported by pairs of ornate brackets show a strong Victorian influence. The upper window sash contains six-over-six panes. The architraves are surmounted by heavy stone cornices, and the central window is further embellished by a crest depicting a fleur-de-lis representing Romain's background and the Cross of St. Andrew representing the union with Esther Ann Chis-

holm. The French windows on the ground level, once sheltered by the protective verandah, are a common Regency feature. The doorcase encloses a large transom light and sidelights, while a broad architrave consisting of ribbed scrolls and acanthus leaf brackets flanks the stout door. Beyond the vestibule, with an identical door surround, a wide staircase gently ascends to the second storey of the wing and then up again to the second storey of the main structure. Beautifully crafted pairs of stately heads support decorative arches at both the upper and lower entry to the staircase. The whole is softly illuminated by a coloured glass light set in a deeply panelled projection on the roof.

Two drawing rooms constitute the south side of the house that once overlooked the bowling green and the lawns that ran down to the lake. A sliding double door connecting the two rooms is set in a handsome architrave capped by beautifully carved brackets that support a bold cornice. Each parlour was warmed by a fireplace with identical marble mantelpieces, each decorated with a grapevine pattern and deeply sculpted cornucopia of fruit as a central motif. Central ceiling medallions of unbelievable complexity and deeply moulded cornices grace every room, but perhaps the most exuberant example of plaster work is exhibited in the dining room where the deeply ribbed cornice and frieze is a fanciful design composed of bananas, apples, and grapes. Apparently when W. S. Davis purchased the house, all the fruit was painted in gaudy life-like colours. Whether the many embellishments that adorn the building are the result of great enthusiasm or lack of restraint is a matter of opinion. Even though it may be described as eclectic for its variety of architectural influences, the Romain House is still the most impressive residence in Oakville.

61

Circa 1856
The Clark-Rose Cottage

308 WILLIAM STREET

William Dalmage Jr. in 1839 purchased the lot at the corner of William and Reynolds Streets from William Chisholm. Although his father William Dalmage was a local tavernkeeper, young Dalmage and his wife Harriet lived in Port Dalhousie, where he was listed as a yeoman. It is probable that he purchased the land as an investment. Nine years later he sold to another investor, William Jones, a merchant in Elgin County. As a merchant and coming from out of town, one of the few men that Jones would be certain to come in contact with would be R. K. Chisholm. Consequently in 1856 when he decided to sell, Chisholm agreed to purchase the property from him for £ 50. Within a month he in turn sold the quarter-acre lot to Isaac Clark for £100.

The document pertaining to this sale describes Isaac Clark as a "joiner." Consequently he was endowed with sufficient skills to erect and finish this splendid frame cottage. It seems that Isaac would have had little time to enjoy his home, for within six years, in 1862, he died in his mid-thirties of smallpox and left the property to his brother Joseph. Joseph Clark had been one of the trustees who established the Congregationalist Church in 1842 and in 1865-66 was a Private in the First Oakville Rifle Company. Clark farmed eighty acres in the 2nd concession, Trafalgar, where the Ford Plant is located today, and let the premises at 308 William out for rent. The Collector's Rolls of 1873 and 1874 tell us that Joseph Clark rented the dwelling in those years to Joseph Boon, a bricklayer. The taxes were $9.10 per annum. The house passed in 1899 from him and his

wife Eleanor to Arthur Clark. Arthur was a farmer in Trafalgar Township, and he also let the house out until he and his wife Margaret sold to Hugh Strathnairn Hamilton Rose for $1,700 in 1905.

Born in Scotland, Rose reportedly led an adventurous life which began when as an infant he was kidnapped by the aborigines in New Zealand. He was a descendant of a noble Scottish family and received a regular income from overseas. Lord Rose, as he was known, and his wife Mary Agnes O'Neil, a native of Cobourg, lived by the lake in a house at the foot of Trafalgar Road before purchasing the Clark house. Lord Rose died in 1905, shortly after the acquisition of the cottage, but his wife lived on there with her sister and niece for a number of years. In the early 1920s Agnes Rose married Daniel Sullivan of Peterborough, and their summers were spent on the lakes near that city, while winters were spent at 308 William Street. The house was rented to Thomas B. McQuesten from Hamilton and his sisters who resided at Whitehern during the remainder of the year but enjoyed summers in Oakville. The Clark-Rose Cottage has changed hands numerous times over the years, and an almost equal number of additions have been made to the dwelling, but the classic proportions and beautifully executed millwork in the main part of the structure have happily endured. The hip roof and three-bay front are characteristic of a simple Ontario cottage and can be seen in a similar building across William Street built by carpenter John Gallie in 1854. The two buildings are laid out on completely different plans, but the most marked difference is that

the Clark-Rose Cottage is blessed with an unusually impressive doorcase. The projecting cornice, deep frieze, and pilasters are all remarkably simple in design. Similarly, the large transom light, side lights, and four-panel door are not uncommon, but the total result is most dramatic when flanked by the two large, well-proportioned six-over-six windows. The central hall with principal rooms on either side leads to an extremely large dining room. Both front rooms have access from the hall and from a bedroom behind, and each bedroom has access to the dining room, resulting in a traffic pattern that relieves the flow through this large centrally located room.

Although the plan is basically symmetrical, the south easterly corner of the house once accommodated a well-stocked pantry where now a passage leads to a bedroom wing added during the early 1970s. It was probably in 1905, when Rose purchased the cottage, that the stylish, stamped-metal ceiling so popular at the turn of the century was applied in the dining area and in the front hall. The kitchen is in a tail at the rear of the main block. Beyond the kitchen and a step down, lies the summer kitchen. Miss Ella McDermott, a grand-niece of Mary Rose, recalls that during the time her mother lived there a maid occupied a small room at the rear of the summer kitchen.

This house will probably be forever known as Rose Cottage, for even though he died soon after its purchase, there are few homes in town that can boast "Lord Rose slept here."

Circa 1856
The Custom House

8 NAVY STREET

When William Chisholm, as Customs Officer, appointed his third eldest son, Robert Kerr Chisholm, Deputy Customs Officer, he deeded to him the block of land where the Custom House now stands. Chisholm had already established a general store on that property and it was suitable for adaptation as a Custom House. The twenty-year-old Robert, or R. K. as he was called, lived on the second floor, above the business operation, and when his family moved into the building, after losing their home in a fire, he moved the Custom operations to a small frame building close by.

On his father's death in 1842, R. K. assumed the post of Customs Collector, and in 1846 he appointed Anthony Dixon as his assistant. Dixon was paid a salary of £15.6.9 per annum. In 1846 the gross revenue derived from the Customs Collections amounted to £ 410.12.5½. The volume of grain, timber, and other goods shipped to the United States increased at a rapid rate until in 1850 the revenue reached £1,472. In that year, Oakville was declared a "Warehousing Port," and Chisholm erected a storage shed to protect the goods in transit from the elements. The warehouse was erected on the bottom land at the foot of the eastern pier. In 1851 Joseph Milbourne succeeded Dixon and received £75 per annum. The salaries of Customs Officers were in a ratio to the amount collected by the port and the length of service of the officer, hence the increase in Customs

revenue during the 1850s was reflected in Milbourne's salary of £100 in 1855.

The need for larger premises to house the Customs service was long overdue, and finally in 1856 the two-storey brick structure at the foot of Navy Street, the Custom House, opened its doors. The new building contained two offices, the front one for the Custom House and the rear office, opening onto Navy Street, for a bank. The first branch of the newly founded Bank of Toronto occupied this space, and on July 20, 1857, the Manager John Burnside made the following announcement: "This institution has now commenced business and will allow interest at the rate of 3 percent on current accounts, and the rate of 4 percent on permanent accounts." Burnside occupied the apartment on the second storey of the building where his sister acted as housekeeper. Burnside's stay was not long, however, as the Bank of Toronto closed down in the depression of 1860.

The Customs operations occupied the front portion of the building, and for the use of these premises the Government paid an annual rental of £ 22.10. R. K. Chisholm, who had served as Deputy under his father's charge, acted as Customs Collector for fifty-two years until in 1894 he was forced by illness to resign his post after a total of sixty years of duty. He was succeeded by Captain Maurice Felan, a retired mariner, farmer, and businessman. Felan was followed by a suc-

cession of other Collectors when the operations were transferred from the Custom House on Navy Street in 1910. Finally in 1937, after 103 years, Oakville was declared no longer a Port of Entry.

When it was in operation, almost one-third of the ground floor of the building was taken up by two large brick vaults, the walls of which were two-and-a-half feet thick. Upon entering the bank from Navy Street, customers were confronted by a long, black walnut counter and the double iron doors of the vault. A stove stood along one wall, and from it a pipe rose up through the high ceiling to enter a chimney on the floor above. Burnside reached his apartment by a long staircase that climbed up the outside of the building, but now an interior staircase rises from the rear of the structure.

Visitors entering the Custom House from the south side found a long panelled counter stretching the width of the room. Massive S-shaped pedestals supported the heavy mahogany top. In front of the iron door to the vault stood a cashier's cage, fashioned of finely turned balusters. The north wall was virtually covered, floor to ceiling, by a great mahogany dresser containing drawers and cupboards and a myriad of pigeon holes. A marble mantel similar to those in the adjoining residence, where R. K. lived, enhances a fireplace on the westerly wall. Today no remnants of either the bank or the Customs

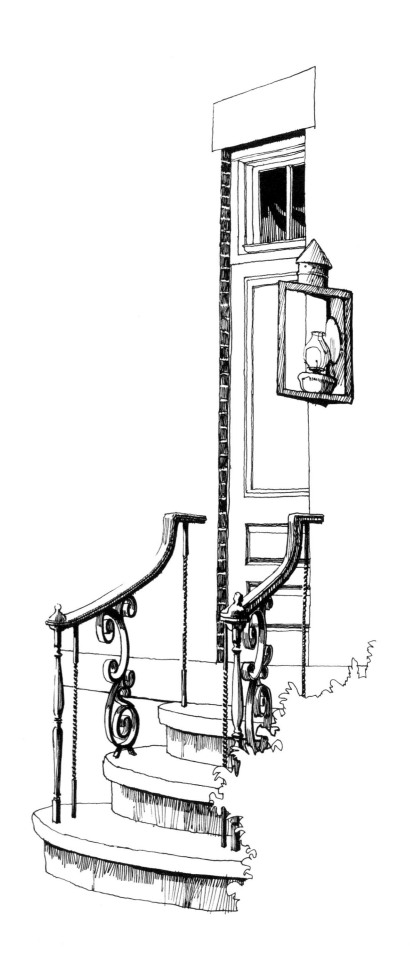

business remain, although little alteration was required to convert the structure into a private dwelling.

The Custom House was built on the plan of the Classic Temple, with the gable-end towards the front and the main entry, rather than centred, set in one of the side bays of the façade. This side-hall plan is characteristic of the Classic Revival or Greek Revival style. Set upon the low hipped roof, gables with deeply recessed brick pediments crown the entry to both the Custom House and the Bank. A simple cornice surrounds the structure and the over-all design is clean and uncluttered. Red bricks brought over as ballast from Oswego are laid in a common bond pattern on a foundation of limestone which had returned as ballast from Kingston in the grain schooners. A dressed stone drip course, sills, and lintels are subtle refinements on an otherwise simple building. The original blinds still hang by the large six-over-six window openings. A large transom light is set within a starkly simple door surround on both entries, but a graceful curving railing welcomes visitors to the Custom House door. It is hoped, with the acquisition of the building in November 1977 by the Town of Oakville, it will continue to welcome visitors.

Circa 1856
The Granary

103 ROBINSON STREET

As the dense bush in the north of Halton was gradually cleared and the new land opened up, the pioneer by-products of lumber and potash were replaced by wheat and flour in the burgeoning agricultural economy of 1850. Grain was shipped across the lake to New York State and overseas to Britain to satisfy the needs of these areas that had converted too rapidly to the lure of industrialization. Because Oakville was so ideally situated on the lake, its excellent harbour acted as a funnel for the grain harvests of the rich farmlands to the north. The eager farmers carted their grain in open wagons to the port of Oakville, where an ever-ready flotilla of hungry schooners waited to be filled. The grain shipments from the port of Oakville reached their peak in 1856, when more than 280,000 bushels were shipped to the United States in that year.

The general merchants of early Oakville not only sold manufactured goods but all manner of produce as well. Consequently these merchants were regular customers of the pioneer farmers. Two local merchants, William Francis Romain and Peter Archibald MacDougald, were sufficiently enterprising to see the opportunities in this trade, and in 1854 Romain took MacDougald into his business. Two years later they joined the row of merchants who were already operating grain warehouses along the east bank of the Sixteen. Land Registry records note that in 1856 R. K. Chisholm and Thompson Smith, who owned the saw mill and lumber yard on the west bank, sold the land where the Granary now stands to Elijah Williams, James Belyea, and Alexander Douglass. These three gentlemen may have been responsible for the erection of the Granary solely as an investment. They rented the premises to Romain and MacDougald, whose names have long been associated with the building. The possibility of a later date for the building's beginnings is minimal, as the grain tonnage dropped off drastically after that date.

Unlike the majority of grain storage houses which were flimsily erected wooden sheds, Romain and MacDougald operated from a utilitarian structure that was masterfully functional yet of classic proportions and implemented by highly skilled carpenters and masons. Cut into the steep side of the bank, the stone walls of the Granary measure as much as two feet in thickness. They were constructed of lakestones brought up by stone-hooking boats from off the Oakville shoreline and of limestone from Kingston brought as ballast in the returning schooners. In addition to arched lintels over two door openings, dressed stones provided formal lintels and sills on the other openings, permitting the remaining wall surface to produce a contrasting random pattern. Massive pine timbers frame the interior and provide support for the expansive roof. Other than the twentieth-century window sash and doors, the only display of exterior wood trim is a simple cornice and frieze, the ample proportions of which are commensurate with the sturdy dimensions of the structure.

Measuring 34' × 73', the building consists of three full storeys and a loft. The lower level, buried deep in the bank, is at grade level on Water Street which at the time also served as a tow path along the river's edge. At one time the lower level was divided into horse stalls, and the names of some of these horses still remain on the ceiling beams. Heavily laden wagons were drawn up to the east end of the building, where an earthen ramp, similar to that on a banked barn, led up to the third floor, where the principle of gravity took over the bulk of the physical work. The grain which generally arrived loosely piled was taken from the wagons, measured, and poured down chutes to the storage bins on the floor below. These bins were lined with stout tongue-and-groove pine boards. From the second level a trestle projected westerly out over Water Street to the water's edge. A hopper or barrow dumped the grain from the trestle into the hold of the waiting vessel.

The Granary owners were perhaps a few years late to have fully capitalized on their investment. By the time the warehouse was in operation, the flow of wheat had already begun to diminish, for with the arrival of the railroad the farmers in the north had a more accessible mode of transport for their produce. Within a few years, the Romain and MacDougald partnership was dissolved and Romain retired his interests in the disappearing local grain trade. It appears that Mac-

Dougald continued to utilize the building, for in 1869, Registry documents indicate that he purchased the property in that year from two other investors, Thomas Paton of Montreal and George Taylor of Hamilton. MacDougald held the property until 1880, when he sold it to his son, William King MacDougald, who four years later sold it to his mother. Mary Jane MacDougald sold the property in 1887 to John Wales, flour-and-feed merchant, who in 1894 also purchased the Grangers' Warehouse which was later to become the Oakville club. Thereafter the property changed hands several times before Hugh C. Pullen purchased it in 1943 after lengthy negotiations with owners in England.

Although a portion of the building had been outfitted as an apartment, the structure had generally fallen into a state of extreme decay. Pullen, who purchased the building to house a light manufacturing enterprise and as a warehouse for his products, undertook major renovations and by these efforts saved the building from collapse. Loose and rotting joists and supports were repaired and the roof reshingled, but unfortunately the eave returns were sufficiently rotted to justify their removal. Metal louvres, similar in appearance to the originals, replaced the old wooden ventilators on the long side walls. Small windows were cut into the top of both gables, and the other openings were glazed at this time as well, to replace the heavy plank interior shutters that had previously been the only light and air control. Pullen removed the earthen ramp from the east wall and added ground floor doors and an emergency staircase on the north wall. Hugh Pullen installed a furnace and chimney in the building at this time, and was probably the first individual in the Oakville area to attempt to utilize the mechanical heat pump principle. Unfortunately the copper tubing buried in the ground around the Granary froze solid the water lines of a neighbouring residence and the ambitious experiment was abandoned. The Pullen business flourished, and when after ten years additional space was required, the old building was vacated. Ownership then changed several times, and since the mid-1960s the fate of the Granary has been most uncertain. Although it is neither a splendid residence nor a grand public building, it is an excellent example of a very functional structure of another era—and it is the only remaining stone granary on the lake. At the time of writing its final disposition still hangs in the balance.

Circa 1857
The Donald Campbell House

293 MacDONALD ROAD

Born in Scotland, Donald Campbell was a member of the contingent sent out to Upper Canada during the Rebellion. Upon receiving his discharge from the Argyle and Sutherland Highlanders in 1842, Campbell chose to settle in Oakville. Shortly thereafter he met and married Jane Laing. The records of the Presbyterian Congregation, of which he was a founding member, note that by 1847 Donald and Jane were married, Jane's mother Mrs. Laing was living with them, and their three daughters, Jane Ann, Jamesina, and Elizabeth, were already born to them. These records also list Donald Campbell as a tailor during the years 1847 and 1849, and with few exceptions this was his usual occupation.

When the sixty-mile plank road stretching north from Oakville to Fergus was built under the auspices of the Trafalgar, Esquesing, and Erin Road Company in 1850, it was deemed necessary to install toll-gates in order to offset the costs of maintenance and repairs. Toll gates were eventually established every few miles along the plank road, and Donald Campbell was given the position of keeper of the toll-gate where the Sixth Line meets Trafalgar road.

The Collector's Rolls of 1853 note that Campbell was a tenant in that year; however, in November of 1856, he became a land owner. Donald Campbell (or Douglass Campbell as he signed the document) purchased from John A. Chisholm, as part of his Survey, a lot at the northwest corner of MacDonald Road and Reynolds Street for £100 or approximately $400 in the currency of the day. Campbell took out a mortgage for the sum of £125 in March of 1857, and it is most likely that his home was completed in that year.

The Presbyterian records note that their daughter Jane Ann Campbell was a teacher and that she joined the congregation in 1868. Within a few years she married William Street, mariner. Captain William Street was a charter member of the Independent Order of Odd Fellows and a Mason. During his career on the lakes, William Street acquired several lots in the John A. Chisholm Survey, and in 1873 he and his father-in-law, Donald Campbell, purchased the lot adjoining Campbell's property. On the deed, Campbell was listed as a tailor, but two years earlier, when well into his sixties, he described himself as a carpenter. In March of 1882, George Sumner noted in his diary: "In the p.m. I went to old Douglas Campbells funeral."

Three years later, Sumner wrote: "I was up this p.m. to see Wm. Street who is very sick." This was one of many such visits Sumner made in the next two weeks and with great sadness he reported on April 29, 1895: "Will Street died this A.M. 10:30 was up to help lay him out—tis so sad and a good fellow." Two days later he added: "was at Will Streets funeral he was buried with Masonic honours. There was a fine turnout headed by Howarths band. Every thing went off well under the Mastership of W. Ferrah."

Jane Ann and William Street had two young daughters and two sons, and with his untimely death at age forty-three, it appears that Jane Ann lived on in the house with her mother. Jane Campbell died within two years, leaving Jane Ann to raise the four children and support herself by teaching school. Jane's and William's two daughters never married and the house remained in the possession of the Campbell-Street family for almost one hundred and fifteen years.

The new owners acquired the property from the family, and although the interior has been dramatically altered, they have carefully preserved the exterior of the structure. The Donald Campbell House is a side hall entry on a six-bay front. The windows have retained the original six-over-six sash as well as the original shutter blinds. The addition of a one-storey board and batten tail to the rear of the house was most sympathetic to the character of the building and appears as an integral part of the growth of the original stone tail. The two-storey front façade is unique in that it displays a fine pattern of Flemish Bond with a cornice of decorative brick work and brick returns at the eaves. The remainder of the second storey is faced in brick as well; however, the lower storey at the rear and on the two sides, like the foundation, is constructed of roughly laid river stones.

Circa 1857
The Murray House Hotel

75 NAVY STREET

Until the arrival of the railroad in 1855, the existing hotel accommodations in Oakville were sufficient to cope with the stage and steamer passengers. In that year John Williams demolished the house then standing on the corner of Robinson and Navy Streets, and in order to service the increased traffic contracted the building of the impressive, twenty-one bedroom, four-parlour Canadian Hotel. In 1861, *The Great Western Railway Gazeteer, Commercial Advertiser and Business Directory* ran the following advertisement: "This house is the best in the place, and open for the accommodation of the public where they will find every comfort desired. Good Stabling attached. Omnibus to and from cars."

The Canadian Hotel became the favourite hostelry in Oakville and was continually filled with travellers and local revellers. Williams served countless banquets and suppers for the Masons, the Orangemen, and the Trafalgar Agricultural Society, and in 1863 he hosted fifty militia volunteers for a grand presentation dinner. Williams sold out in 1866 and the hotel was sold again a year later for $2,005. Thereafter until the turn of the century, the hotel underwent a succession of more than twenty different proprietors and operators. The hotel offered bagatelle boards and oysters and for a time even gave space to a doctor's office. Dr. Ogden's wife was the daughter of the owner at the time, Robert Shaw Wood. Wood sold the hotel in 1875 to J. Anderson, and in the same year Anderson placed the following advertisement:

"Canadian Hotel, Navy Street, Oakville, Ontario. This hotel has been entirely refitted and refurnished and will now compare favourably with any hotel in the province.

Sample rooms and special accommodation for commercial men and every convenience for the travelling public. The bar is supplied with the best brands of liquors and cigars. Dougherty's bus meets all trains and steamboats. Terms, moderate. Good stabling and accommodation for farmers. An attentive hosteller, J. Anderson, pro."

Oddly enough, just three years later he advertised for a "good plain cook."

Two women were the proprietors in 1881 and they caused their neighbour and local constable George Sumner to write in his diary, "The town is pretty quiet if it were not for the Canadian Hotel. They keep up a continual noise — most disreputable for those who profess to be ladies." It is likely that the "drys" were supported by such disturbances when they finally mustered enough influence in 1881 to bring forth a "no whiskey vote." James Taylor, with the backing of the Temperance forces, purchased the hotel for $5,000 in 1886. He lasted just a few years because of financial difficulty, and in 1896, when the Scott Act was repealed, Murray Williams, a nephew of the original owner, purchased the hotel from James Flaherty, giving it his own name. Murray had been a hotel and tavern keeper for some time, and with his resources and business acumen (for a while he also owned the Oakville House), he operated the hotel successfully for the next forty years.

Murray Williams and his wife Henrietta raised seven children in addition to operating the hotel. From the hotel, Williams also raised pigeons and indulged himself in the luxury of an automobile. He was one of the first men in Oakville to acquire a car, purchasing his in 1905, and in 1908 he is reported building "an auto house" on the property. To the south of the building in a small garden, there stood a fine cast-iron fountain topped by a mesh basket ringed by three cast angels. The stream of water emitting from the centre of the basket caused a small white ball to rise and fall before the waters cascaded over the three basins and the supporting swans to the pool below. Murray Williams, the garage, the original wagon sheds, and the barn are long gone. But the fountain has been relocated and the Murray House is still operating.

The structure has undergone major renovations to the interior. However, the exterior still bears a strong resemblance to the hotel depicted in the *Halton County Atlas* of 1877. The Murray House displays faint traces of Greek Revival lines in the low, broadhipped roof, wide overhanging eaves, and a deep, simple frieze. Three square-headed bays break up the expansive wall surface, and like columns they frame a symmetrical arrangement of large windows. Hand-hewn beams span the sixty-foot length of the attic and a row of eyebrow windows surrounds the structure. Variously known as the Canadian Hotel, the International Hotel, and the Murray House Hotel, this is the largest commercial building in Oakville to come out of the nineteenth century.

Circa 1858
Erchless

4 NAVY STREET

In 1836, James King, brother of William MacKenzie King and a ward of William Chisholm purchased that block of land now occupied by Erchless. In 1837 the ownership was transferred to William Chisholm who had a general store erected on it in that year. This brick building, the original part of Erchless, faced north upon Front Street, which at the time ran through to Water Street. Beyond its front entrance, towards the river, was an archway which contained a platform where wagons could unload goods. In 1839 William Chisholm deeded the land and the building to his son, Robert Kerr Chisholm. R. K. received the property and also the title of Deputy Customs Officer. It is thought that R. K. ran the Custom operation from the red brick store and lived there as well. In that same year, William Chisholm's frame house, which had been built at the corner of Lakeshore Road and Thomas Street, was consumed by fire, and he, his wife Rebecca, and the younger children moved in with R. K. The building was enlarged at this time by an addition to the south so that the front then faced on the lake.

Although he was only twenty-three when his father died, Robert accepted the responsibilities of carrying on the family affairs and

immediately assumed the position of Postmaster and Customs Officer. By 1856 he was a prosperous gentleman, and with his business enterprises secure, R. K. Chisholm became engaged to Flora Matilda Lewis, a daughter of Shubel Lewis and Caroline Romain. With the forthcoming marriage, R. K. undertook to have his home enlarged. The Custom Office was by then operating out of a new building he had erected to the southeast, but his mother and several younger brothers and sisters had remained in his house. By February of 1858 the addition was completed for his bride. R. K. and Flora raised four children in the house he called "Erchless" after the

twelfth-century castle in Inverness-shire, Scotland, the seat of the Chisholm clan. Over the years R. K. served the community by acting as Justice of the Peace, Councillor, Reeve, and Mayor. He was Secretary-treasurer of the White Oak Lodge in 1868, the year it was founded.

Rebecca Chisholm lived with her son R. K. and his family until her death in 1865, when she dropped dead at the iron gate in front of the house. For many years Rebecca's bedroom, on the southwest corner of the house, was believed by the Negro servants to be haunted.

The 1861 Census notes that James Bell Forsyth Chisholm and his wife Adaliza and their sons were also living at Erchless. James, born in 1835, was a younger brother of R. K. and grew up in Erchless. As a chemist, he operated a soap factory in a small shed on the shore of the lake. He was also a druggist and for that purpose he maintained a shop on the Lakeshore Road. He married and continued to live in Erchless with his family until his early death in 1868. Thereafter his wife and sons continued to live in his brother's house.

In the last quarter of the nineteenth century, numerous additions appeared on the

grounds. The hill on the river side of Erchless was stepped in a series of terraces. A tennis court was laid out on the bottom land. A boathouse was set upon pilings in the river, and a windmill was erected to pump water from the river up to a storage tank.

R. K. Chisholm suffered a stroke in 1893, and on February 27, 1899, George Sumner wrote in his diary: "Was called up this morning at 3:30 by Ziller to help lay out R. K. Chisholm who had just passed away in his 80th year."

Erchless remained in the Chisholm family and Allan Chisholm, an unmarried son of R. K., lived on at the house until long after the turn of the century. He was responsible for the design of the charming stable and coachman's dwelling at the north end of the property, as well as laying out the planting of the grounds. Allan, a fine sailor and an avid tennis player, was one of the organizers in 1903 of the Tennis Club that later became known as the Oakville Club.

The front garden of Erchless is enclosed by a cast-iron fence, the supporting posts of which are crowned by pineapple finials. A pedestrian gate and a carriage gate, side by side, their latches still intact, open into the grounds. The front façade is a six-bay front

with a side-hall entry. The common bond red brick is accentuated by dressed stone lintels over the round-headed windows. These stone lintels are capped by bold wooden cornices. The window sash contains 13" × 20" glass panes in a six-over-six arrangement. The front doorcase is set back in a shallow umbrage. Wooden panels decorate the side-walls of the recess, and a round-headed transom light and sidelights illuminate the entry

hall. The four-panel door is incised on both sides with a vertical line down the middle to suggest a pair of two-panel doors. Although Erchless displays many Victorian characteristics, this and the side hall entry are both features more common to the Greek Revival style. The two generous parlours on the west side of the main building cannot but impress the visitor with their spaciousness, and this is further enhanced by the generous ceiling height of twelve-and-a-half feet. A wide plaster cornice and a sixteen-inch baseboard surround the rooms. From the broad hall a wide staircase rises to turn at a landing before it rises again to the second storey. Higher ceilings in the latest portion created a change in floor levels between additions. A narrow winding staircase climbs from the upper hall to the attic, where a simple set of stairs leads to a rectangular belvedere on the roof. From behind the low balustrade that encloses the surrounding deck, Chisholm could survey a fine view of the busy port. Today the view is still splendid, as there are more sailing vessels than ever before in the Oakville harbour.

Erchless has been home to six generations of Chisholms, and it is most befitting that the home of the founding family is at last in the possession of the town itself.

Circa 1858
King's Castle

21 REGENCY COURT

Barbara Chisholm married George King who died during the War of 1812. Barbara King died in her twenty-fourth year, but before her death in 1817 her two young sons, William and James, were made wards of her brother William Chisholm, the founder of Oakville. William MacKenzie King, who was born in 1811, left Oakville as a young man, and in the course of a chequered career he sailed to the far corners of the world. King survived two shipwrecks in his travels at the end of which he found himself in the southern United States. Gold was discovered in California in 1848, and there among the thousands of other fortune hunters William King was to find gold and what appeared to be a change of luck. Shortly thereafter he returned to Oakville, determined to settle down, establish himself in business, and become a gentleman farmer.

In January of 1858, R. K. Chisholm, King's cousin, purchased 100 acres of lot 16 in the 2nd concession from King's College for the sum of $700. In the same month King bought the property from R. K. for $2,400. In July of that year, King, who described himself on the document as a farmer, took out a mortgage of £1,250, or approximately $5,000 in 1858, from his other cousin George Chis-

holm. As a subscriber to Tremaine's *Map of Halton County, Canada West*, William King was entitled to have a portrait of his new residence depicted on the border of the map. Although his house was only begun, he commissioned the illustration in 1858, the year Tremaine did his survey.

With plans for a forthcoming marriage on the horizon, it is believed that under his direction construction of the "Residence of W. M. King Esq." was started that summer. The new structure was sited close by a grouping of older brick buildings that had earlier served as a post house and station for changing horses. The buildings comprised a tack room and a rudimentary tavern. They were connected by a long brick wall against which a lean-to roof had been affixed to provide shelter for visitors' horses. The kitchen tail of the new house served as a link with the tavern of earlier days. The new structure bears a strong resemblance to many of the buildings A. J. Downing described as rural Gothic Villas in his book *The Architecture of Country Houses*.

In his journeys, King must surely have seen many such fine dwellings being erected in the United States. Suitably impressed, and with these images in his mind and possibly the plans in his pocket, William MacKenzie

King had a country home erected to express his "refined and cultivated taste." Downing described this class of dwelling thus: "What we mean by a villa, in the United States, is the country house of a person of competence or wealth sufficient to build and maintain it with some taste and elegance . . . we may add that a villa is a country house of large accommodation, requiring the care of at least three or more servants."

John A. Williams, shopkeeper, noted in his reminiscences that King's plans for marriage fell through and that he married his housekeeper. Although King chose the name "Solitude" for his new home, it was to be forever known as "King's Castle." His plans for his new home and his life as a country gentleman also slipped through his fingers, for in 1859 he was required to sell the property to R. K. Chisholm. A month later, in September of that year, R. K. sold it again to one of his brothers, Thomas C. Chisholm. William King's other venture, the *Oakville Advertiser*, a reform newspaper of which he was publisher, continued in operation for only a brief time thereafter. John A. Williams also related that King's aunt "Mrs. Barnett Griggs left him hotel on Navy Street." This is a reference to the Frontier House. The Collector's Rolls of

1866 confirm that Mrs. Griggs was the owner of the house at the time, and it is noted that W. M. King was living there as a tenant. It is evident from Registry Office records that he never held title to the property, and in 1877 he is recorded as a tenant in the house on Forsyth Street owned by saddlemaker Henry Gulledge. William MacKenzie King died in 1879 at age sixty-eight after a difficult life. Although Williams described him as "no credit, no money, no hope," it is difficult not to admire a man who kept looking for success in the face of such adversity.

In 1871 Thomas Chisholm and his wife sold King's Castle to Richard Postans who for fifteen years cultivated vineyards there. A young boy by the name of Cyril Maude was sent out from England to work on Postans farm with the hope that it would dissuade him from joining the acting profession. Exile in the colonies did little to deter the young man's ambitions for Cyril formed "The English Church Theatre" and the troupe performed in the Town Hall. Cyril Maude departed Oakville and his garret room high above the kitchen of King's Castle, eventually to gain theatrical fame as an entertainer during the First World War.

The house changed owners several times and the hundred acres was reduced to little more than six acres when it was purchased in 1897 by Sara McCausland. Robert and Sara McCausland had four children when they purchased their country home. Robert McCausland operated the family business in Toronto which was responsible for designing and crafting some of the finest stained glass and leaded windows in that city. The McCausland firm also installed windows in Knox Presbyterian Church in Oakville and in at least one private residence as well. In 1902, McCausland advertised King's Castle in a publication called the *Garden of Canada*. He described it as a three-storey solid brick residence with thirteen rooms and bathroom, good plumbing, water in the house, and heated throughout by a warm air furnace. He also mentioned a brick woodshed, a brick poultry house (the tack room and tavern), a substantial frame stable, and a carriage house recently rebuilt. Harry Ryrie purchased the property in 1908 and in two years it was sold to William T. Merry, a manufacturer of printing inks from Toronto. The Merrys lived in King's Castle for eight years, and there they raised four children, and on what is now part of the Oakville Golf Club they pastured dozens of ponies. Herbert, who was born in

the house, married Eleanor Nancy Robinson. Mr. Herbert Merry, active in civic affairs, served as Councillor and Reeve for many years.

The property again changed hands several times. For a while it was the residence of the M. P. Mallon family and a summer retreat prior to being sold to Arnold Banfield in 1945. Banfield and his wife Rhea chose the property as the ideal country setting for raising their family that grew to four children. There they operated the Banfield Company, a manufacturer's agency, in the converted stable and outbuildings on the grounds. The local firefighters held numerous practice drills on the steeply pitched thirty-eight foot high roof and these "dry runs" proved most beneficial. When an almost disastrous fire in 1960 destroyed the early "tack room and tavern," it was another fire brigade, however, that saved the day. In place of the ruined buildings, a large one-storey, modern kitchen, games room, and seven-car garage were attached to the dining room—the room that had served as a kitchen in William King's day.

Numerous other contemporary renovations, both exterior and interior, were effected at this time in order to maintain the large premises and adapt it to the busy lifestyle of the owners. Arnold Banfield died in 1961. The business operation was relocated in Toronto and in 1965 King's Castle was sold. A number of private owners and developers held the property until the present owners, Mr. and Mrs. Lawrence Weeks, acquired it in 1973 and embarked upon an ambitious restoration program. King's Castle was the first private dwelling in Oakville to be designated an historic building under the Ontario Heritage Act.

Until the fire, the original twenty-foot deep, boulder-lined well was accessible under the floor of the post house "tavern." It is now sealed under the floor of the new kitchen. Upon the examination of numerous floor plans of "country houses" built in this period, it would seem that the room which now serves as the dining room was originally the kitchen, as this utilitarian room was almost invariably removed from the main block. The rear portion of the house is not so broad as the main part, nor is it a full four storeys high. The considerably lower ceiling height and the less imposing wood trim relegate it to the status of a kitchen tail, even though the two areas appear to have been built at the same time. The existing outbuild-

ings were likely used as a summer kitchen, woodshed, and cold storage room. The kitchen seems to have been transformed into a dining room sometime after the turn-of-the-century, and on that occasion a new fireplace replaced the original and decorative beams were affixed to the ceiling. From the original kitchen a narrow staircase ascends to the servants' quarters and to the garret above.

The marble mantel is gone from the parlour, but five fireplaces remain to add warmth to the living room, the original dining room, the original kitchen, and two bedrooms where the two cast-iron round-headed fire boxes have been left intact. The parlour and dining room are joined by a broad semi-elliptical arch. The arch, defined by a deeply ribbed wood trim and capped with a wooden keystone, once was filled with French doors and a handsome fanlight. A long hall stretches down the north side of the first floor from the main entrance on the east end. A broad staircase with walnut balusters leads from the hall to the second storey. During renovations, evidence was uncovered which suggests that the pine woodwork of the passage was grained to simulate a hardwood. At the same time pencil lines were revealed on the original plaster walls of the hall that would suggest a desire to create a facsimile of ashlar stone blocks.

The Regency verandah shown in the illustration on Tremaine's map is gone, as is the surrounding glass-enclosed solarium of a hundred years later, but the basic form of the structure still conforms to A. J. Downing's description of the "picturesque villa" with its "high roofs, steep gables, unsymmetrical and capricious forms." As Downing says, ". . . the design is in the domestic Gothic or pointed manner." The fanciful pairs of chimneys, the pointed arch windows in the narrow gables, and the splendid bargeboards have endured the many years of change. However, time has taken its toll and the wooden window caps in the form of Tudor labels, and a multitude of other details are gradually being replaced or repaired by the present owners.

The old post house, recorded on a provincial map of 1833, is gone, as is any hint of the old Indian trail that once ran across the north east corner of the property. King's Castle is now securely surrounded by a twentieth-century housing development, and in all probability this noble structure will outlast its new neighbours.

Circa 1858
The Robert Farley House

205 TRAFALGAR ROAD

The land this house stands on was bought by John Wood in 1839 from William Chisholm as an investment. Wood was a mason and later a tavernkeeper in the town of Fergus. On his death his wife sold the land to John Urquart, an Oakville druggist. Urquart held the property for six years and in 1857 sold it to Robert Farley for £50. Farley was listed as a clerk, and it is quite possible he was in the employ of Urquart because seven years later, when he sold the property and moved to Guelph, he too was recorded as a druggist.

One year after Farley bought the land, he and his wife Mary took out a mortgage for £106. It was paid off in 1859, and in 1860 he took out another for the sum of $2,000. This was paid up within three months, and just a month later he took out yet another mortgage for $400. It is not likely that Farley used all this money to make improvements to his home. Possibly he borrowed against his house in order to set himself up in business. In 1864 he and his wife sold to George Rutherford of Hamilton for £300. Rutherford purchased it as an investment, but Oakville was beginning to fall upon slow times and he took a severe loss, selling it in 1867 for approximately £125.

The new owners were Charles and Jerusha Lusk. Jerusha was the daughter of John Potter who had lived just a block north on Trafalgar Road. Dr. Charles Horace Lusk, a physician, was attracted to the teaching profession and served as assistant to the Head Masters of the Public School for many years. Charles and Jerusha had four children. Their daughter Lotta married Herbert Ashbury, son of Thomas Ashbury the miller; one son, Charles, became a doctor who practised in Toronto, and Ross and Egbert moved to Chicago. The family were devout Methodists and Dr. Lusk was instrumental in organizing the building of St. John's Church. The Church records of 1878 state "the Trustees worked from beginning to end without a jar or dispute of any kind, but Dr. Lusk's untiring labours both of body and mind, looking after the interests of the work, should never be forgotten by the Methodists of Oakville." Over the years many church socials were held at the Lusk home, and in 1886 the Sabbath School presented Dr. Lusk with a gold watch for his ceaseless work. A newspaper of 1911 states "Dr. Lusk has passed his seventy-fifth milestone, but still walks as erect as a soldier and attends to his medical practice with unfailing devotion. But it is the Sabbath School of which he has been superintendent for thirty-one years that Dr. Lusk appears to best advantage as an ideal superintendent. Under Dr. Lusk the school moves like well-oiled machinery. He has perfect order. Nobody seems to know how he gets it. He never asks for it, never demands it and rings no bell." Three years after his death in 1920, St. John's paid him their greatest tribute when Dr. Charles P. Lusk, son of Dr. Charles H. Lusk, laid the cornerstone for the new Lusk Hall.

Upon the death of her husband, Jerusha Lusk sold the house to Dr. William Morley Wilkinson. Wilkinson was Medical Officer of Health and Coroner for Trafalgar Township. He too was a member of St. John's Church where he was made an honourary elder. Wilkinson served on the Board of Education, was a recipient of a Fifty Year Pin from the Masons, and received a "Citizen of the Year" award from the Lion's Club. He and his wife Janet had four children. Janet Wilkinson died in 1953, and their daughter Mary was married from the house just prior to its sale in 1954 to the Bramalls.

The asymmetrical Farley House with its side-hall entry embodies many characteristics of the Gothic Pointed style. A deeply sculptured tin medallion distinguishes the steeply pitched gable. The windows of the second storey are of the original casement type, while those of the first floor were resashed around the turn of the century. The central Gothic window on the gable had been shuttered on the exterior and plastered over on the interior until the present owners purchased the house from the Wilkinsons. Fortunately the entire sash and glass were found intact within the wall. Similarly the other upper window on the west wall had been closed over, and a window on the south wall in the parlour below is still plastered over and shuttered. A red ochre paint wash with false mortar lines masks the original brick work of the main structure.

Intricate fretwork once formed a decorative bargeboard at the eaves, but now only the stout bracketed porch with cutaway scrolls remains. A verandah running along the north wall once led patients to a waiting room and an office that served both Dr. Lusk and Dr. Wilkinson. This office is now a den, but at one time a pass-through window in the wall gave access to the dispensary that consisted of a lean-to shed on the tail. The large room on the south once had a decorative arch to partially divide it into a parlour and dining room. A one-storey brick tail originally served as a kitchen before it received a second storey and a covering of clapboard. This area became the dining room and the kitchen was pushed back further as the tail grew.

The new owners have made several additions, including a studio, and all have been in character with the structure. All reflect their enjoyment of the house. The Robert Farley House is perhaps better known as the Lusk House, the Wilkinson House, and more recently the Bramall House.

Circa 1859
The Henry Gulledge House

142 FORSYTH STREET

In 1835 Henry Gulledge of Somerset, England, landed in Upper Canada. As a young man of twenty-one, he was faced with the same momentous decision that must have confronted many immigrants. Henry had to choose where in this new, broad land to set up shop and carry on his trade of saddlery and harness-making. After considerable deliberation, Oakville's bustling harbour and growth potential won out over Toronto.

From his shop on Lakeshore Road, now number 190 East, Gulledge fashioned beautifully crafted harnesses and fine leather saddles. A harness set from Henry Gulledge could cost £3.5, but the obliging Henry could be counted on for six months' credit. In 1836 Gulledge purchased a lot at the corner of Forsyth and Rebecca Streets from Forsyth and Richardson, a Montreal trading and investment company. Church records of 1847 list Gulledge as a vestry man in the Parish of St. Jude's and in the Census of 1851, Henry and his wife Maria are recorded as having six children. Maria died in 1854 at age thirty-eight. Three years later Henry took out a mortgage of £100, and it is quite likely that he used this money for the erection of the house on Forsyth Street. According to the Census of 1861, a two-storey barn sheltering a horse, a cow, and a pig stood on the property behind the Gulledge house.

Two of the Gulledge boys learned the trade of harness-maker under their father. By 1869 George, the elder, was already a very professional craftsman working in New York State, and it was there that Henry sent his youngest son, Edmund, after he had served his apprenticeship. Edmund put in his internship in Jamestown and there honed his skills. On his return Henry took in the young man, now nineteen, and made him a partner. In 1877, at age twenty-five, Edmund bought his father's interest and expanded the business which, in 1875, had moved back to the site of his father's original store. He now sold such ready-made items as boots, shoes, and trunks. The enterprising Edmund prospered. He became a sizeable landowner and for a time served as Town Councillor.

In 1873 Henry took out a $250 mortgage against the house and property. It is not certain where Henry was living but in 1885, at age eighty, he is recorded as a grocer. It is possible he had earlier entered into business with his daughter, Mary Anne Moulton, who for many years operated a candy shop and grocery store.

When "Hy" Gulledge died in 1899, his son-in-law Captain George Moulton purchased the house from the estate for $175. Moses Tyrrell, a gardener for the C. W. Marlatt estate, rented the house in the 1890s. Moses and his wife Sofia had nine children, one of whom recalls that even then the house was beginning to slide into disrepair, as the stucco coating that covered the clapboard siding had begun to fall away. This one-and-a-half storey structure is of a size and plan that was common in early Oakville. As the modest home of a tradesman, it grew as its many contemporaries did with the addition of a lean-to across the rear creating a salt-box design. This additional space served as a kitchen and probably in the last quarter of the century replaced a smaller tail that initially served the same purpose. 134 Thomas Street, the home of shoemaker John Brown, is an almost identical twin to the Gulledge home, and it still bears evidence of a staircase in one of the front rooms. It is most likely that the Gulledge staircase also rose from one of the front rooms, but with the addition to the rear it was more suitably situated and later enclosed.

Even though little in the way of architectural details grace this simple structure, the scale, pleasant proportions, and tidy appearance impart a warm welcome. Maria Gulledge never lived to see the house. However, her tombstone, after being replaced by a larger monument, survived several moves around town, where it acted as a back stoop and a patio stone, and finally came to rest in the backyard at Forsyth and Rebecca.

Circa 1859
The Moses McCraney House

549 LAKESHORE ROAD WEST

William McCraney, one of the earliest settlers in the Oakville area, was born in 1762 and is variously reported as having come from Rhode Island, New Jersey, and New York State. He was documented, however, as a blacksmith, and he arrived in Upper Canada in 1801 with his wife Eunice and three children. They first settled by the Grand River but with the opening up of Trafalgar Township McCraney petitioned for land and drew a lot on the north side of Highway No. 5. Preferring to live nearer the lake, he leased, in 1807, the Clergy Reserve, lot 19 in the fourth concession below Lake Shore Road. One year later he purchased two hundred acres in the third concession above Lake Shore Road. He also leased the adjoining land in the Clergy Reserve, lot 19 in the third concession comprising also two hundred acres. In a report of Clergy Reserves by Deputy Surveyor Samuel Wilmot in 1829, William McCraney is listed as owner of lot 20 in the fourth concession. This parcel consisted of sixty acres, sixteen of which were cleared, the remainder being wooded in pine, maple, oak, and chestnut. This property was valued at twenty shillings per acre. It is not surprising that the junction of Lake Shore Road and the 4th Line became known as "McCraney's Corners."

William and Eunice had twelve children but only six were to survive childhood. William died in 1829 and was buried beside his wife in the family plot in the east corner of the farm. Their son, William Payne McCraney, who was born in 1803, took over the lease of the 200-acre Clergy Reserve in the third concession, and in 1840 he purchased the easterly half of this lot for fifteen shillings an acre, a total of £75. William Jr. married Rebecca Teeter and they had their first child, Moses, in 1823. When William dropped dead at age forty-seven while working in the fields, Moses, being the oldest son, inherited the farm and all the other McCraney holdings which he divided among the other members of the family.

Sarah Thompson and Moses McCraney were married in 1858 and the couple moved into the family homestead on lot 20 in the third concession. The old house was destroyed by fire shortly after they moved in, causing Moses and Sarah to move into a two-storey carriage house that stood at the rear of the old house while their new house was being built. The carriage house also included a "machine shop" where their oldest son was born, according to a grand-daughter of Moses McCraney, Ysobel McCraney Green. When the building was demolished after the turn-of-the-century, Sarah's attempt to make it more homelike could be seen in the scraps of wallpaper still clinging to the walls. The Census of 1861 records that Moses was living in the "stone house" at that time. A kiln for firing bricks was situated on the farm and it provided a reasonable business, but his interests were drawn first to the general merchants shop he operated in Bronte and then later in Oakville. By the early seventies Moses had moved his family into a house in town, 213 Trafalgar Road. It was here that a son, Franklin George, was born in 1872, father of Ysobel. Moses' Oakville business was destroyed in 1883 by a fire that threatened the entire commercial district. In 1889 Moses, his wife, and two sons moved to Toronto where he invested in nine houses in various locations around the city. Three years later, at age sixty-one, Moses McCraney died, and in 1902 his son Franklin, who operated a coal business in Toronto, returned with his wife Grace and their daughter to the family farm.

Two other children, Helen and Foster Murray, were born in the old house during the time that Franklin tried his hand at farming the homestead property he named "Olden Holme." In addition to apples, in one year, 1913, the McCraneys picked and shipped twenty thousand quarts of small fruits to Toronto, Montreal, and Winnipeg, and even with the many hired hands the work load proved too heavy for the ailing Franklin.

In 1909 John Guest, son-in-law of Sir Edmund Walker of Toronto, visited Oakville while looking for a site for a boy's private school. In that year Appleby College purchased a portion of the land south of the Lakeshore Road that had once been held by the McCraneys from Judge Colin G. Snider, and within two years building of the school had commenced. John Guest became the first Headmaster. Franklin and his family were tired from the rigors of farming and in 1913, with the school enrollment already quite large and not all the building complete, he rented the old homestead to the school and moved the family to California.

Appleby College acquired the property when Grace McCraney died in 1923, but in that first year thirteen boys, a housekeeper, and a master squeezed into the old Moses McCraney House. Raymond Massey and Wilder Breckenridge were two of those boys.

The McCraney House served as a boarding home for many boys over the years, and more latterly it has served as a residence for school masters and their families. In the process most rooms were at one time sheathed in a tongue-and-groove wainscoting, the house was divided, the original staircase was moved to the east and another staircase was added to the west. New windows had been cut into the east and west walls of the second storey but fortunately the other windows have retained their original sash. The large 10″ × 18″ panes are set in a six-over-three configuration on the upper storey and a six-over-six on the ground floor. The windows are deeply recessed in the fourteen-inch-thick walls, and only the stout wooden sills project. The walls are of a rubble stone and cement mixture coated with several smooth coats of stucco. The surface has been scored to simulate ashlar blocks, and lines of black paint to suggest mortar strips may still be seen on the warm cream-coloured stucco. A stucco-coated drip course protects the lakestone foundation. A four-panel front door, once surmounted by a transom light which has since been covered over, is flanked by a pair of sidelights that are almost the height of the door.

To all who pass by, the Moses McCraney House presents a warm, friendly air and gives a feeling of solidarity and strength. One hopes that this example of a Regency farmhouse will endure to harbour many more generations of Appleby boys and masters.

Circa 1860
The William Gamble House

60 REBECCA STREET

Lot number five at the corner of Rebecca and Wilson Streets was in the possession of Robert K. Chisholm in October of 1859 when he gave a mortgage to Thompson Smith, a lumber merchant, for the sum of $289. It is most likely that the house was built on the property shortly thereafter, and that it was erected solely as an investment. In 1873 Smith discharged the mortgage to R. K. Chisholm, who like himself was an entrepreneur and developer, owning many properties around the town. In 1877 Carter Whiting is recorded as a tenant, and a well cover bearing the date 1879 confirms that the structure existed at that time.

In 1886 Chisholm sold the property to glove manufacturer William Gamble for $300. Gamble, who was listed as a "glover" in the Collector's Rolls of 1894, was in the leather business and either worked at the Marlatt & Armstrong tannery or operated one of the smaller tanneries that periodically attempted to compete. The elaborate plaster decorations were possibly an attempt on Gamble's part to enhance the dwelling and make the interior more attractive for his bride-to-be. William Gamble, aged sixty-three, born in England, was recorded as a widower when he married Hannah Lucas, a widow, in his home on Rebecca Street in October of 1891. The Reverend W. E. Graham of St. Jude's Church performed the ceremony. In 1912, at age eighty-four, Gamble, again a widower, died leaving the house to his sister Maria Gamble Filby. She and her husband were Steward and Stewardess of Trinity College in Toronto, and over the ensuing years many eminent

clergy stayed at the house on Rebecca Street. When Filby died in 1920, Mrs. Filby's niece, Florence, came out from England to care for her, and upon Mrs. Filby's death a tablet covering the graves was placed in St. Jude's cemetery bearing the inscription: "Sacred to the memory of Edward Edwin Filby, born 1846, died 1920, who for over twenty-five years served faithfully as steward at Trinity College, and his wife Maria Elizabeth Gamble, born 1837, died 1933. This stone placed by the Corporation in grateful remembrance of their loyal devotion to the interests of the College." Florence married William Wills a few years after her arrival in Oakville, and the couple lived in the house for many years after Mrs. Filby's death.

The William Gamble House exhibits many characteristics of the late Regency style; the hipped roof, the pebble dash stucco wall surface, and the large window openings. The delicate spindles and fretwork on the porch, and the unusually high siting of the structure above grade level, however, are more characteristic of the Victorian era, while the two-over-two window treatment is a turn-of-the-century improvement. An innovative mind has adapted the window shutters on the north side of the house by replacing the louvres with glass so that they may serve as storm windows. A simple transom light and blinds embellish the doorway. The main floor consists of four rooms. An impressive, semi-elliptical ribbed arch divides the two principal rooms on the east, and the ten-foot ceilings are bordered by a strongly moulded cornice. The walls were judiciously divided

with the application of decorative panels by William Wills, who was a painter and decorator. A narrow staircase, with a walnut handrail, handsome newel post, and finely turned balusters, centred on the back wall of the house, leads to the lower level. This area also comprises four rooms. The largest one was panelled by Wills with a dark oak wainscoting. Three steps lead up to what was once the kitchen. This addition was clad with tree bark at one time, and the roof of the house was sheathed in tin. A long verandah similar in design to the entry porch sheltered the north side of the house and was removed when the Town of Oakville expropriated land for the widening of Rebecca Street in 1962.

Outwardly the William Gamble House is a simple dwelling, but inside it is richly embellished with many architectural refinements found only in residences of far greater physical stature.

Circa 1863
The Captain William Wilson House

390 LAKESHORE ROAD EAST

Born in Ireland in 1811, William Wilson arrived in Upper Canada with his parents and his two brothers, Robert and George, when he was eight years old. They settled near the Head of the Lake, and at an early age William signed up on a sailing vessel to commence his career on the lake. William and his brother Robert married sisters from the neighbouring village of Port Nelson. The Census notes that William and his Scottish-born wife already had one child by 1841. In that year William is recorded as renting property in the town of Oakville. Because of his wife's Scottish ancestry, the Irish-born Wilson joined the Presbyterian Congregation in 1848 with his wife and two young sons.

In 1849 William Wilson was listed as Captain of a schooner out of Oakville. This position rewarded him handsomely, and within six years time he had a large three-storey brick commercial building erected on Lakeshore Road. For many years, John McCorkindale, a general merchant, occupied the building, and since that time it has served numerous other merchants, the most recent being a florist.

William purchased lots one, five, six, and nine in the newly laid out Thompson Smith Survey in November of 1862. The *Plan of the Town of Oakville* published by Michael Hughes in 1863 shows that the house, now 390 Lakeshore Road East, was standing on

the lot that year. The same map shows that Wilson also owned two lots on the south-east corner of Reynolds and Sumner Streets, and one on the north-east corner of Reynolds and Church Streets by 1863. Predeceased by his wife, William Wilson died ten years later, in December of 1873. In March of that year he drew up his will, and it is evident from what he bequeathed to his children that in the intervening years he had acquired a good deal more real estate.

Wilson's only daughter, Mary Jane, was left four lots in the Thompson Smith Survey, including lot number one "on which the Brick House and Barns are situated" and "my cows, sheep and household furniture." His son, Robert, was bequeathed five lots in the Thompson Smith Survey, including a lot immediately east of the family house. Robert also received a lot in the Town of Orillia, and in addition he was left "the eight-day clock in my dwelling house and the Horse, Buggy, Waggon, Sleigh, Cutter Harness and other appendages thereto." His son, Thomas, was given six lots in the Survey and a lot in Orillia. His other son, George, had previously received a large sum of money, consequently Wilson left George's wife, Ardelia, one lot in the Thompson Smith Survey.

Mary Jane Wilson left Oakville for Toronto and later moved to Chicago. Her brother Thomas had moved to Pennsylvania and

Robert was in far-away North Dakota. Mary Jane rented out the house until 1890 when she sold it and "other lots" for $2,200. Edmund Gulledge owned the property for a year before he sold it, and after Gulledge a long list of owners and landlords followed. In 1930 the house was purchased by Mrs. Bessie Cook who duplexed the building, creating two apartments. In 1944 Herbert Merry and his wife purchased the house and had it divided into a triplex. A portion of the Wilson House was rented for many years to the Marriott family until it was purchased in 1973 and converted back to a single family dwelling. Subsequently the house had two other owners before the present owners took possession.

The William Wilson House is a square-plan structure. It displays a hipped roof side-hall entry on a six-bay front. Two large windows on the first storey are set on a dressed stone sill at floor level. They consist of a six-over-six pane configuration; the individual panes measuring 8¾" × 19". At one time the brick-work of the front façade received a red "wash coat" and an artificial grid of mortar strips were mechanically applied to the renewed surface.

The main block comprises a front hall and staircase and a front parlour which is separated from a spacious dining room by a wide opening. The opening once contained a pair

of French doors. A small sitting room adjoins the dining room on the west. The original kitchen tail was replaced by a two-storey brick addition not long after the house was built, and the lower floor of this tail now houses the new kitchen and utility rooms. The east wall of the dining room is dramatized by one of three early fireplaces. The mantel of the fire opening in the living room has disappeared and only the surrounding tiles remain, but the fanciful Victorian mantel in the dining room survived unaltered. Two French doors flank the fireplace and lead to an enclosed porch. The doors comprise fifteen panes and each door is surmounted by a transom light.

The upper storey shows extremely plain baseboards and door surrounds. In the front bedroom a pair of square windows with equally simple surrounds are set just two feet from the floor and are of a three-over-three pane configuration. The second floor of the tail is several steps down from the main block of the house. The room in the addition displays a unique fireplace. A small cast-iron mantel in the best of the late Victorian style is mounted on the south wall. Measuring 3'9" × 3'6", the exquisite mantel encloses a fire opening of a mere 2'2" × 1'4".

When William Wilson had this house built in 1863 he incorporated several architectural features unique to Oakville. It seems that the unusual window proportions and placement were design elements he had seen in his travels as a mariner. Similarly, the distinctive mantels were in all likelihood purchased on a trip to the United States.

Circa 1865
The Captain Edward Anderson House

148 WILLIAM STREET

In that first decade, when Oakville was struggling to become more than just a settlement, a handful of men lent an air of dignity to an otherwise wild land. Edward Anderson was such a man. He was already a landowner when he purchased for £25 the lot on William Street from William Chisholm. A few years later, in 1837, he was described as a "gentleman" when witnessing a document for James McDonald. As a gentleman he was obviously retired and was of some means. The lot on William Street was very likely purchased as an investment. Edward Anderson died in 1840 and was survived by his wife Sarah Anne and their son Edward.

Edward, heir to his father's estate, took out a mortgage for the sum of $200 in 1865. In 1866 the Collector's Rolls record Anderson as owner, but the building appears to have been incomplete at the time the roll was taken. In 1867 he rented the completed dwelling to George Morden. Anderson was the captain of a steamship, but because the Oakville harbour was no longer the busy centre of commerce it had been in the forties and fifties, he sailed out of Toronto.

Anderson paid off his mortgage in 1868 and it is probable that he married his wife Lucretia at this time and moved into the house, for a year later he added onto the structure. His neighbour George Sumner, as well as being Town Constable, supplemented his modest income by practising his former occupation of carpenter and attached the addition to the Anderson house. The addition was a lean-to shed that was drawn up from a neighbourhood building and affixed to the rear to create a large kitchen. Sumner records in his diary that he purchased the shingles and other

lumber at Lee's Planing Mill from a fifty-dollar budget, and that "ten square of shingles cost $17.50 for use on E. Anderson's house."

The Andersons had four children but only one lived to adulthood. When at the age of six their son Frank drowned in the Sixteen Mile Creek, Edward, upon receiving a telegraph in Toronto, proceeded to walk home for the burial. In 1872 twin boys were born to them, but George was the only survivor. In 1875, the Andersons had a sale of furnishings and left Oakville for Sarnia. Their daughter died in 1876 shortly after the family had moved from town. Anderson telegraphed Sumner "to get a grave dug and have the hearse at the station for his little girl, Flora." They rented out the house for five dollars a month and four years later sold it to Thomas Mulholland, a machinist. He in turn sold the house to Thomas Howarth in 1886 for $725 cash.

It seems that Howarth bought this modest house because he had most of his money tied up in his business, a private bank. In addition to being a banker, Howarth was Secretary and Treasurer for the Town and headed the Oakville Citizen's Band. Led by Howarth and his violin, many an impromptu concert took place on William Street. In 1902, when the Andrew & Howarth Bank failed, the distraught Thomas Howarth took his own life. According to Sumner, "Howarth was buried today with Masonic honours. The Foresters turned out too—had the Oakville Band. It was a large funeral—many teams." In 1913 his widow Mary sold the property and somewhat later it came into the hands of W. S. Davis, a staunch adherent of St. Jude's

Church. He donated the house and land to the Church to serve as the sexton's residence, as it has done to this day.

The Anderson House is almost identical to five other houses in the town. All are of the same proportion and basic plan. All have a similar central gable on the front façade with a round-headed window and all seem to have been built in the 1860s. The two houses on Trafalgar at the corner of Randall replaced the old Halton County Hotel in the mid-1860s. 247 Trafalgar was built in 1869 when a fire destroyed the house that had previously stood there. Examples of this Oakville vernacular can be seen at 31 Reynolds and 312 Randall Street. The Reynolds Street building still retains some of its Victorian bargeboard decoration, but the fine fretwork on the Randall Street house has disappeared.

All the windows on the Captain Edward Anderson House are round-headed save for two on the rear of the tail. The window architrave is deeply moulded, and although the sash has been replaced the original shutter blinds remain. Apart from the windows the only other detail is a fine beading on the bargeboards and corner boards. The porch, compatible in design with the structure, is not original and was added after the last rough cast stucco coat was applied.

The interior is equally simple, with the exception of the later addition of a richly embossed tin ceiling in the parlour. Popular at the turn of the century, this was probably an attempt by Thomas Howarth to add a touch of finesse to a pleasantly proportioned but otherwise plain structure.

Circa 1870
Potter's Folly

241 TRAFALGAR ROAD

John Potter was born in Nova Scotia in 1811 and came to Oakville as a young man where he found work as a carpenter on the piers. Within a short time he was working as a shipwright for William Chisholm, and it was not long before he was building houses as well. John Potter and his wife Elizabeth had two daughters, Mary and Jerusha, and the records report that Potter and his family were renting a house during the 1840s. The Census of 1851 states: "John Potter, joiner, born Canada, W. Methodist, age 42, Framed House, 1 storey, 1 fam. occup. wife Elizabeth, ch. Mary E. and Jerusha." The Collector's Rolls of 1852 list Potter as a tenant on lot 3 of block 44 as Charles Biggar as the owner. Biggar had purchased the land (now 241 Trafalgar Road) from William Chisholm in 1839. It has been suggested that Potter was given the contract to build a small frame house on the lot, similar to the Melancthon Simpson House, and then rented the house from Biggar for a number of years before purchasing the property.

In 1842 Potter was responsible for the construction of the Congregationalist Church that stood at Wilson and John Streets, a large frame structure, capable of seating 150 persons. He was a member of the Oakville Temperance Reformation Society, and in 1843 he was one of the men instrumental in the construction of the Temperance Hall. In 1852 John Potter is listed as a member of the Oakville Mechanics' Institute, and in 1857 and 1858 he served as a Councillor for the new Town of Oakville.

From his shipyard on the Sixteen, Potter launched many illustrious sailing vessels. The most notable were the *Smith and Post* which he built for Thompson Smith, the 100-ton schooner *Kate* for George Chisholm, and the 175-ton *Dauntless* for Captain Hiram

Williams. By 1859, however, Potter was in financial difficulties, and he sold his home on Trafalgar Road to Thompson Smith "subject to certain trusts, creditors being parties of fourth part." In 1861, Thompson Smith, assignee of John Potter, sold the property to Solomon Savage who on June 1, 1869, sold to John Barclay and Peter MacDougald. On Sunday, June 20 of that year, just nineteen days after the purchase, Barclay and MacDougald lost the house to a fire. George Sumner wrote in his journal: "This afternoon Mary Maneer and Potters old place was burned to the ground. The wind blew very hard."

Although the earliest known record of the present building on the site at 241 Trafalgar Road is in the Collector's Rolls of 1874, it is believed that Barclay and MacDougald contracted the start of the building shortly after the fire. The newly completed building was rented to the Presbyterian Congregation, and there is evidence that the Reverend William Meikle was well ensconced in "the Manse" by 1874. Meikle has arrived in Oakville six years earlier to minister to the Presbyterian Congregation. The church was undergoing alterations at the time and services were held in the Temperance Hall. At a social in aid of the building fund, the *Canadian Champion* reported that "Mr Meikle appeared to appreciate the good old games of our grandmother's days, as highly as any in his flock, and participated in the sport of 'forfeits,' blindman's buff, etc., without any ostensible compromise of his clerical dignity." Fourteen dollars was realized for the fund from this social, and Mr. Meikle was elected to the position of vice-president of the Temperance Society in that year.

Exactly how the building became known as Potter's Folly is not certain, and although

there is no proof for the supposition it is possible that Barclay and MacDougald let the building contract out to John Potter. Potter never lived in it, and according to the Collector's Rolls of 1874 he was a tenant, living with his daughter Jerusha and his son-in-law Dr. Charles Lusk, at 205 Trafalgar Road. He was still living there in 1888 and it is believed he lived there until his death. In his later years he listed himself as a boat-builder, and although he was obviously still active he was not affluent. In 1892 and again in 1899, George Sumner recorded in his diary that he had been up to visit old Mr. Potter who was quite weak and on January 8, 1908, Sumner wrote, "Old Mr. John Potter died this am in his 98th year."

The Presbyterian Congregation bought the property in 1881, and numerous other ministers dwelt there over the years, with the Reverend Mr. Wallace being the last to reside in the Manse. The property and three adjoining lots was sold in 1927 to William Robert Adamson of Toronto. Adamson died just two years after the move to Oakville, but in that time he became very involved in the operations of Knox Church as a member of the Board of Managers. In 1939 his wife Ethel became the first woman elected to sit on the Board, and she remained a member for eight years. Ethel Adamson served Knox Church in various capacities for over forty years, and in 1966 Ethel and the late William Adamson were honoured by the presentation of a stained-glass window to the church. One of their four children, William James Adamson, was ordained in 1948 into the ministry at Knox Church, Oakville.

The Adamson family remained in the house until 1945, and a number of families have owned the property since that time. The house has undergone various alterations over

the years, and in 1978 the new owners John and Amy Griffiths had the structure jacked up and moved forward sixty-five feet on the property to permit a new, full basement to be built and the sale of lots on Reynolds Street. Today, the Presbyterian Manse, or Potter's Folly as it is more commonly known, sits a little closer to the street than it did before, but its fanciful character has remained intact.

A. J. Downing, an American nurseryman *cum* architect *cum* writer, did more to influence the taste of mid-nineteenth-century America than almost any other individual. In his book *The Architecture of Country Houses*, he describes what could be Potter's Folly:

"Roof rather flat, and projecting upon brackets or cantilevers, windows of various forms, but with massive dressings, frequently running into the round arch, when the opening is an important one (and always permitting the use of the outside Venetian blinds); arcades supported on verandas with simple columns, and chimney-tops of characteristic and tasteful forms. Above all, when the composition is irregular rises the campanile or Italian tower, bringing all into unity, and giving picturesqueness, or an expression of power and elevation, to the whole composition."

This structure is the only example of an Italianate Villa in Oakville. The balconies on the tower are gone and the tent-shaped verandah with its fine treillage has been replaced by an enclosed sitting room. With the closing in of the porch, an entrance was created from the principal room on the north. The room must, however, have been very dark, for some time later a pair of windows were cut into the north wall, one on either side of a closed-up fireplace. The drawing room on the south side displays a simple fireplace on the east inside wall. The ceiling is

almost ten feet high, but the great height is reduced by a picture rail that surrounds the room. The baseboard is simple but fifteen inches in depth. A vestibule receives visitors to the front door and draws them into a long foyer where the stairs rise in a long flight to a landing where they turn and rise again. A staircase also rises from the rear of the kitchen to the servant's quarters. The area over the kitchen and the adjoining sun room was considerably altered by Mr. Adamson prior to occupying the house in 1927. The roof was raised three feet and the floor level was raised to correspond to the floor level of the second storey of the main part of the house. A large upper hall at the top of the main staircase measures 13'6" × 10'9" and provides access to three large bedrooms and a lesser room over the vestibule. The two bedrooms on the south side are set several steps up from the hall, and the ceilings are higher than on the north side. The larger room measures 16'6" × 13'6" and is festooned with a plaster picture rail formed in a delicate rope and tassel design.

The small room under the tower is but seven-foot square, and here knife-edged glazing bars define the double window. A steep set of stairs (now gone) once rose to the trap door in the ceiling and into the tower room. The tower room, with bare pine floor and unfinished walls, commands a spectacular view from the four sets of round-headed windows.

As an architectural style, the Italianate Villa was popular throughout the third quarter of the nineteenth century in Ontario, and designs for such could be found in countless builders' pattern books. It seems as if one such structure was erected in almost every town of consequence, but often as not only one.

Circa 1873
The Captain Francis Brown House

289 TRAFALGAR ROAD

Born in England in 1842, Francis John Brown went to sea at an early age. Drawn by news of the discovery of oil in the western counties of the province, he came to Canada. Brown arrived in Oakville in the summer of 1867 and according to the Collector's Rolls he was renting the old brewery on the bank of the Sixteen, north of MacDonald Road, in that first year. In 1868 and 1869 Brown was listed as a brewer, and it is likely that he operated the brewery for a year or more before he purchased the business and named it the Victoria Brewery.

Francis Brown married Hannah Moore shortly after his arrival in Oakville. Hannah was the daughter of John Moore, the mariner, and Sally Griggs Moore, the daughter of Barnett Griggs. The Browns had the first of their six children in 1868. In 1870, the year Francis was confirmed in the English Church, a depression started to close in on the town, forcing him to shut down the brewery.

By 1871 Brown was already describing himself as a shopkeeper, and according to an advertisement in *The Argus* in September of 1873 Francis J. Brown was well established. "Notice—Parties desiring their winter's supply of coal must leave their orders for the same at Brown & Heiter's store." In that same year, Brown is recorded as a merchant and owner of the schooner *Meteor.*

In 1873 Brown was a tenant on park lot F which was located on the north side of Sheddon Avenue between Reynolds and Allan Streets. The property was registered in the name of Jane Moore Heiter, his sister-in-law. In 1874 he was again registered as a tenant in a dwelling owned by Mrs. Heiter, but the dwelling place was given as 289 Trafalgar Road. This land, known as park lot J, had earlier been owned by Barnett Griggs, and

when he died in 1864 his will was contested, leaving ownership of the property in a state of considerable dispute for many years. As the daughter of Barnett Griggs, Hannah Brown and her husband Francis were involved in several exchanges before he was granted the property in 1870. He then sold the land to Mrs. Heiter who took out a mortgage for $1,000 in 1873. It would seem that under Brown's direction the house was erected over the following year, even though he was still officially a tenant and Mrs. Heiter the owner. According to Registry Office records, the property came back into his possession in 1882, where it remained until 1896.

In 1879 Francis Brown was given the commission of a steamer for the route between Canada and England, whereupon he returned to the sea. His journeys later took him to Africa and in 1880 he sailed to Japan. Brown's travels so impressed the local people that George Sumner was given sufficient cause to write in March of 1882: "F. J. Brown gave a lecture on his voyage around the world—had a full house—free!" Brown continued to sail in the Orient and over the years he shipped and brought home a vast collection of rare and beautiful bronzes, ivories, embroideries, and china vases. On his return in 1889 a supper was given in his honour at the Murray House Hotel—"a big crowd and had a good time." In this year Brown held the first exhibition of his collection at his imposing residence on Trafalgar Road. With this first display of curios and art, Brown began his "Oriental bazaar."

Many families have lived in the Francis Brown House since the turn of the century, and numerous changes have been made to the structure, but none has affected its dramatic appearance. The long tent-shaped verandah that shaded the front of the house

is gone, as are the narrow widow's walk and low balustrade that surrounded the belvedere high upon the hip roof. The front entry has received a new door surround, but the patterned transom light, the casement windows, the shutter blinds, and eighteen-inch stucco-covered walls are just as Brown knew them. The stout walls were constructed of random beach stones set in a thick mix of mortar within a wooden form. When the mortar had set, the forms were moved and the process repeated. The east wall now has been included within the new kitchen tail by the present owners, and the stucco surface was removed to add a most interesting wall texture and at the same time reveal the composition of the walls themselves.

Erected on a central hall plan with two principal rooms on each side, the house originally had a frame kitchen tail. The dividing wall between the two parlours on the north has been removed, and a large stone fireplace was installed by the Root family after 1920. Earlier, a brick fireplace was installed in the front room on the south side by the Madden family between 1910 and 1920.

Because of the thickness of the walls, the window sills are correspondingly wide. This substantial appearance is carried through in the deeply sculptured baseboards, door and window architraves, the panelling beneath the windows, and the ceiling cornice. An oak handrail and finely proportioned balusters form a handsome staircase rising from the front entry to the second storey where there are four generous bedrooms. A smaller room at the top of the stairs has a trap door in the ceiling, where another set of stairs once gave access to the lantern on the roof.

The Captain Francis Brown House is one of those rare cases where a widow's walk did provide a vantage point for the waiting wife.

Circa 1875
The Captain John Andrew House

114 CHISHOLM STREET

John Andrew was born in Dundonald, Scotland, in 1846 and as a youth emigrated with his family to the Canadas. The Andrews settled in Oakville where John and his brother James took to the lakes at an early age, each earning a reputation as master mariner and highly respected lake Captain.

In 1867 the Assessment Rolls listed James Andrew as the owner of lot 6 in block 63. In 1871 John Andrew purchased the surrounding lots 5 and 7 in that block from R. K. Chisholm and his wife. The Assessment Rolls of 1874 record that the John Andrew property had not increased in value, however, in December of that year he took out a mortgage of $400. The house was erected the following spring on lot 5, for in 1877 the Assessment Rolls show William Anderson as a tenant, John Andrew as owner, and a $400 increase in the assessment. The property was transferred back and forth many times between John and his widowed mother until in 1884, at the age of thirty-eight, he married thirty-three-year-old Isobella Evitt and the house was registered in her name. It is not known if John lived in the house at 114 Chisholm, as he also owned a house that at one time stood directly behind the building. The Collector's Rolls of 1888 record that brother James Andrew was renting 114 Chisholm in that year. James had given up sailing in the early 1860s to acquire considerable fame as a builder of lake schooners and steamers in his shipyard on the west bank of the Sixteen Mile Creek. There he produced vessels for the local Doty Ferry Company and the Toronto Ferry Company, as well as building many of the most famous racing yachts ever to sail Lake Ontario. These included the *Aggie* for Armstrong and Marlatt, which he built in 1887, and the *Canada* in 1895. Both of these yachts enhanced his reputation as a builder of Canada Cup stature.

James Andrew continued to produce the fastest, sleekest sloops and cutters on the lake until as an old man, in 1925, he sold the shipyard. James and his sisters, who shared the house with him, moved from 114 Chisholm Street in 1891, when John and his wife sold the property to William and Sarah Cornwall. The Cornwalls held the property until 1903 when they sold to Walter Russell. Russell, a widower, remarried shortly after purchasing the house. His new wife, Myrtle, was much younger than he. When Walter's grand-daughter, Gladys, was deserted by her father, a freighter captain, Walter and Myrtle took in the child and raised her as their own. A small lean-to was attached to the rear of the pantry to serve as a bedroom for the child, since there was little room to spare for Myrtle also took in boarders. When Myrtle Russell died, the house was passed down to Russell's grand-daughter Gladys, Mrs. M. D. Forbes, who had grown up in the house. The property has remained in the family since 1903 and has been a home to five generations.

Originally clad in a weatherboard siding, the Captain Andrew House wears a coat of pebble dash stucco. The gable end presents a very basic doorcase and simple window sash to the street. This simplicity is pleasantly relieved by an imaginative fretwork barge board, cut in an unusual chain-link pattern. It is interesting to note that John Andrew was one of the original members of the Independent Order of Odd Fellows. The lodge was formed in 1874, a year before the house was built. A three-link chain is the symbol of the fraternity, and it bears a strong resemblance to the bargeboard design. The side hall entry of the front façade opens into a hall with an attractive staircase with staggered pairs of rectangular, slightly tapered balusters. The 8'9" ceiling height of the first floor is matched by a corresponding head room on the second storey and makes only a minor concession to the sloping gable roof over the three bedrooms. Beyond the front parlour, a generously proportioned dining room stretches across the width of the structure. A door provides entry to this room in each corner; from the hall, the parlour, to a small sliproom at the rear, and to a large lean-to kitchen that runs across the west wall and southerly beyond the limit of the main structure. A verandah traverses the south wall and provides a covered entry for an exterior door to the kitchen, as does yet another verandah to the west. The side verandah is supported by chamfered columns and embroidered in a sturdy fretwork pattern. The kitchen still retains its original four-panel doors and box locks, as well as such turn-of-the-century memories as tongue-and-groove wainscoting, a tongue-and-groove china cupboard enlosing an early enamel sink, and a matching cupboard with built in flour bins.

The Captain Andrew House has endured remarkably well with a minimum of changes and virtually presents an *in situ* appearance.

1877
St. John's United Church

135 DUNN STREET

Justus Williams, a merchant and building contractor, was one of the driving forces behind the establishment of the first Methodist Church in Oakville. Regarding the mid-1830s he wrote: "At that time, there was no place to worship Almighty God but the schoolhouse, which was used by all church denominations." In 1835, a building committee was formed consisting of William Hatton, Robert Leach, and Justus Williams. A site was purchased on the northwest corner of Thomas Street and Lakeshore Road and a cornerstone was laid in that year. When the white weatherboard 36' × 60' structure with its 100-foot tinned spire was completed in 1840, it was the second Methodist Chapel in Upper Canada to be surmounted by a steeple and a bell. Heated by a woodstove and lit by candles, the Wesleyan Methodist Chapel was capable of seating three hundred persons. Unfortunately, the congregation ran into difficulties and was forced to sell the church to the Bishop of Toronto after less than one year. The old schoolhouse was to serve once again as a place of worship for the Wesleyan Methodists.

Ten years later they had rallied and were again eager to build their own church. A Board consisting of Joseph Kenny, Robert Leach, John Potter, Thomas Jull, Solomon Savage, Hiram McCraney, and David Lebarre was set up and a subscription list was circulated. Anglicans, Presbyterians, and Catholics all made contributions to the building fund. A frame 36' × 40' structure was erected on the land at the southeast corner of Randall and Dunn Streets which they had purchased in 1851. The congregation grew in number, and within a few years it was necessary to add a gallery on three sides. By the time the gallery was completed in 1857, the membership numbered 442.

By the early seventies the congregation again felt the need for larger premises, and in 1875 the Reverend Thomas Howard set the wheels in motion. The new Board of Trustees comprised William McCraney, William Young, John Potter, John A. Williams, C. W. Coote, Dr. H. Lusk, Isaac Warcup, William Wass,

John Ion, Alexander Coote, James McDonald, Thompson Culham, Charles Culham, W. H. Cronkrite, and William Savage. By February 1877, $2,000 was raised by subscription and the old church was sold for $400 to John A. Williams to be converted into three stores, with the understanding that the church would be preserved on another lot until the new building was completed. Smith and Gemmall of Toronto were engaged to prepare plans and specifications, and preparations were made to transport materials to the site while the snow facilitated travel.

John Alton contributed the sand from his farm and it was drawn down by volunteer labour. Isaac Warcup gave seventy-eight cords of stone that had been drawn up by stone hookers from the lake bottom. Bricks were supplied by Edwin Brown at $8.20 per thousand, and the stonework, bricklaying, and plastering were done by John Heatley. One of the trustees, William Savage, also recorded that the carpentry work was done by James McDonald Jr., and the seating was fashioned by Robert Shaw Wood in his planing mill. John Cowton was responsible for painting the interior and upholstering the pews.

The main body of the church measured 71' × 45' and a building in the rear, measuring 66' × 43', housed the Sabbath School. The Gothic structure of polychrome red brick with white brick bands and decorative courses was capable of seating eight hundred and with the use of draw seats could accommodate one thousand persons. Gallerys were mounted on three sides and, as there was no chancel, the pulpit stood on a raised platform in the middle of the church with the choir and organ behind, occupying space in the lecture room and separated by a wide archway. The cornerstone was laid in July of 1877 with two thousand people in attendance, and by January of 1878 the church was ready for dedication. On the thirteenth of that month Dr. Ives of New York preached to a full house, and at the close of his sermon he revealed that the church, pipe organ, sheds, and fence cost $14,000, $6,000 of which was

provided for. The remaining $8,000 was to be raised by subscription before dedicating the house to God, and in little more than two hours all was subscribed.

George Sumner wrote in his diary in 1884 of the "amalgamation of the C.M. Church, Episcopal Methodist, Primitive Methodist and Bible Christian Churches." On June 1 he wrote, "We were at church this morning. This is the first Sunday of the union of the Methodist Churches." Over the years St. John's has been the scene of countless fowl suppers, recitals, lectures, garden parties, and great comings and goings as recorded by George Sumner. On July 12, 1903 he wrote, "The Orangemen & veterans of the Fenian Raid marched to the Methodist Church" and on the thirty-first of that month, "The Methodist Sabbath School went on the 'Niagara' to Toronto & Island."

In 1914 subscriptions were raised to provide for alterations and repairs necessary to the upkeep of the building. The galley was cut back, and a new pulpit was donated by Tillie Sumner's Sunday School class, new chairs were contributed by Rebecca Wass' Ever-Faithful Bible class, and new pews were installed. The pointed-arch windows were originally of frosted glass and four stained glass windows were requested at this time. Shortly after the war a large memorial window was installed in memory of the fallen to add further to the beauty of St. John's. An addition was erected in 1923 at a cost of $35,000 to replace the old Sabbath School. This new area was named after Dr. Horace Lusk, superintendent of the Sabbath School for many years. The rear doors of the church were changed to accommodate a central aisle, and the wings of the gallery were clipped back further during alterations of 1939. Ten years later extensive remodelling was again undertaken. Increased Sunday School facilities, a full chancel, a Casavant organ, new heating, an enlarged narthex, and additional seating were among the alterations completed in 1953 at a cost of almost ten times that of the original structure.

Circa 1878
The Joseph Boon House

288 WILLIAM STREET

The lot at the corner of Trafalgar Road and William Street was purchased from William Chisholm by shopkeeper Justus Williams in 1837. Two years later Williams sold it to the Reverend James Musgrove. The vacant land remained with the Musgrove family until 1874 when it was purchased by Joseph Boon.

When they were in their mid-twenties, Joseph Boon and his older brother Isaac sailed from Devonshire, England, for Canada. They were both stone masons by profession; however, as little stone work was being executed in this part of the country and brick dwellings were on the rise, they turned their hand to brick-laying and plastering. The Boon brothers worked together and were the builders of many homes in Oakville, as well as of the Market Building or Town Hall for which they were awarded the contract for both the brickwork and the plaster work. During the 1860s Joseph purchased the Royal Exchange Hotel and was responsible for doubling the size of that structure.

Joseph Boon did not build immediately on the lot at Trafalgar and William, as the Collector's Roll lists him as a tenant in Rose Cottage at the east end of the block in 1874 and again in 1877. In the latter year he also acquired the lot directly to the east, between the two corner lots. In October of the same year he took out a $400 mortgage and commenced construction of the dwelling the following spring. In 1879 he purchased a third lot to the south at the corner of Trafalgar and King Street. The Collector's Rolls of 1879 list Joseph Boon as "freehold, Block 29, A B & D 1200 assessed." The three lots would have had an assessment value of approximately $600, leaving the other $600 to suggest that the house was standing or at least under construction at the time. Certainly the brick tail, set slightly off-centre at the rear to accommodate the large round-headed window in the gable, was a later addition as the brick work indicates.

Joseph Boon and his wife Susannah had five children, two sons and three daughters, and all were born long before the house was erected. The Collector's Rolls of 1894 record that Joseph Boon, age sixty-seven, and his wife were living in the house, and that both were adherents of the English Church. Boon still owned lots A B & D of block 29 and A was built upon but B & D were still vacant. His property was assessed at $1,050 for A and $300 each for B & D for a total of $1,650. Boon was a member of the Council of the Town of Oakville for twelve terms between the years 1872 and 1891. In 1903 Joseph Boon, by then a widower, sold the house and other lots to W. S. Davis who purchased the property as an investment.

The house is basically square in plan with a central gable accenting the front and rear. Each gable contains a round-headed window to correspond to the other round-headed windows on the second storey. The windows on the main floor have segmental heads and the sash is square-headed with two-over-two panes. The bargeboard on the small gables consists of a series of incised droops with discreet pendants and a finely pierced pattern decorating the eaves. The front entry is illuminated by a transom light over what appears to be a door of later vintage with ten glass lights. Other than the transom light, the only decorative elements on the entry are the very functional front door shutter blinds. From the central hall a wide doorway opens into a parlour on the left, with a white marble mantelpiece and cast-iron grate with a base

burner. A pair of French doors lead through to the dining room beyond. A small sitting room with an exit to the sun porch and a vestibule with a staircase to the second floor take up the westerly side. Other than the dining room, the rooms are not large. However, the 9'9" ceiling height and the foot-high baseboards lend an impressive scale to the interior. A sun roof off the dining room also takes advantage of the westerly exposure. This dining room probably served as the original kitchen, until the one-storey brick tail was added by Boon not long after the main body of the house was completed.

The westerly and northerly walls of the structure were at one time given a red wash coat of paint mixed with sand, and then a new set of mortar strips were superficially applied to the surface. This treatment was given to the walls most affected by the foul weather in order to protect the soft red bricks. It is also very likely that this work was done by Boon and that he may have been responsible for this nineteenth-century attempt at brick preservation on several other brick structures in Oakville.

Circa 1878
The William Wass House

457 LAKESHORE ROAD EAST

When, one hundred years after it was laid, the St. John's Church cornerstone was opened and the box removed, an un-listed article was discovered inside. It was a sepia photograph of William Wass, the man responsible for collecting items to be enclosed in the cornerstone. On the back of his photograph he had written "William Wass, son of Noah and Rebecca Wass of the County of Lincoln, England, born there March 23 1817. Emigrated to Canada during the summer of 1852, settled on a farm which I bought on the back concession in Trafalgar Co., Halton, and remained there until January 1857 when I with my wife Mary Wass and my daughter Rebecca Wass removed to Oakville and I have been ever since and now am in business there. Dated at Oakville this 2nd July 1877."

The *Halton Atlas* of 1877 described Wass thusly:
"He has always had a busy life, and has carried on the business of auctioneer, land and estate agent, stock and money broker, notary public, commissioner, conveyancer, accountant, and also farming operations, and has been very successful. He has for many years been an acting magistrate, and has taken a leading part in politics on the Reform side. In religion he is a member of the Methodist Church of Canada."

In 1860 William Wass purchased a one-hundred-acre farm on the east edge of Oak-ville. Today it would encompass the area bounded by Lakeshore Road, Allan Street, MacDonald and Chartwell Roads. Here Wass built a modest dwelling which served as the Wass home until 1878 when he sold all but seven acres. Wass moved the old house around the corner to the north on what is today Balsam Drive. He then contracted William Lee to erect a large and impressive home that would better reflect his successes. Excerpts from the agreement dated April 26, 1878, between Lee, a builder and planing mill operator, and William and Mary Wass demonstrated why Wass was indeed so successful:

"The sum of two thousand eight hundred and fifty dollars of lawful money of Canada to be paid by the said parties of the second part. . . . execute and perform all the workmanship and labour necessary and furnish all the scaffolding and all the materials of first class quality of every kind required in the erection and finishing of a Dwelling House Addition, cistern and plumbing on lot number Eleven in the third concession. . . . further agree to finish and complete the said works for which he has contracted and deliver the same so complete on or before the Thirtieth day of August next AD 1878 under a forfeiture or penalty of Twenty Dollars as liquidated damages for every week the work remains unfinished after the above Time. . . . the sum of three hundred dollars when the stonework is all complete and the cellar drain put in. Three hundred Dollars when the Frame is up and all boarded in and sheeted.

Two hundred Dollars when the outside is all lathed and the Roof and Cornice is finished ready for plastering. Four Hundred Dollars when the floors are all laid and outside of the Building finished and cistern built and finished. Four Hundred Dollars when Plastering and Cornice inside is all finished and windows put in. Four hundred dollars when the Joiners work is all complete and finished and the remaining sum of Eight hundred and Fifty dollars when the whole works are completed finished and delivered."

The Specifications for building the Wass House ran to many handwritten pages. An examination of but a few items reveals a gentleman of impeccable taste and an artisan who took great pride in a job well done.

"Excavation . . . cellar to be excavated to the depth of four and a half feet from average level of the ground and dig trenches for all foundation walls two and a half feet deep and one and a half feet wide. The coal bins to have the earth all taken out to the depth of the foundation that is two and a half feet deep. The Privy vault to be excavated three feet deep. . . . Stonework . . . the cellar wall to be 18 inches thick and 6 feet 6 inches high from cellar bottom to joists . . . and all the stone to be good quarry or lake stone. . . . Cistern . . . excavate for and build a Brick Cistern 10 feet diameter and 6 feet deep clear of arch built of good hard brick circular form wall 8 inches. . . . Lathing and Plastering . . . all of the outside of the building to be lathed with the best lath and plastered with 2 coats of the best Mortar made from the best clean sharp sand and fresh burnt lime and neatly blocked off . . . and the outside plastering to be all of one colour when finished, all interior walls and ceilings to be lathed and plastered

2 coats with the best hair mortar and straightened to ground angles all to be plumb and straight all finished with Guelph white lime and plaster and finished in the best manner of workmanship and materials.''

The plans of William Wass and his builder Lee changed sometime after this agreement was drawn up. During the seventies, a house of this magnitude was invariably fashioned of brick or at least of stucco with ashlar block markings as described, but for some reason Wass changed his mind and had the structure sheathed in a finely milled cove siding.

''Cornices . . . neat cornices to be run on ceilings of Dining Room, Parlour, Library, Upper and lower Hall. Pattern to be approved by the Proprietor. . . . Centre Pieces of the proper size for the different rooms and to be put up in the Lower Hall, Library, Parlour and Dining Room. Centres not to be rim circles but composed of leaves etc. put up in sections. . . . Carpenters and Joiners work . . . The building to be framed in the style known as Balloon frame, studs, floor joists and ceiling joists to be placed 16 inches from centres . . . the first floor joists 3 × 10, the second, joists 2 × 12, ceiling joists 3 × 6 rafters 3 × 6. All inside studding 2 × 4 sized and straightened. . . . Roofing . . . sheathed with sound square edged inch boards laid close and covered with first class sawn shingles laid on a coat of good hair mortar ⅜ inch thick laid 4½ to the weather and well nailed with Fourpenny Nails and no shaky shingles to be used on the building. . . . Front Door . . . to be a sash door glazed with one made up stained glass as formed on plan by proprietor to select pattern, the side entrance door to be glazed with

common glass and frosted. The fanlight over the front door to be stained glass to be approved by proprietor. . . . Doors throughout the building to be 4 panelled and double moulded, the doors in main Building first floor to be 7'6" × 3 ft. . . . Stairs . . . half space landing . . . and walnut rail, newel and Ballusters, turned in the best style and pattern . . . back stairs with oak rail and oak ballusters. . . . Privies to be fitted up as shown on plan with white earthen basins. . . . Bath Room . . . to be provided with tank 2' × 4 ft. 3 feet deep of wood lined with tin.''

The bathroom in the Wass House was originally situated on the second floor in the tail where the staff lived. It was reached through a door on the landing of the stairway. Because the ceiling height in the tail was a foot lower than the eleven foot height in the front part of the house it was necessary to descend several steps to reach the rear hall.

''Painting and Glazing . . . all woodwork inside (except floors) to have 2 coats of James white lead and oil. . . . Blinds to be painted 2 coats lead and oil and 2 coats of the best Paris powdered Green. . . . Front door and panelled jams to be grained oak. The roof to have two coats of fire proof paint a slate colour. The proprietors to furnish Mantel Pieces and Grates for fireplaces.''

The mantelpieces chosen by Wass further demonstrated his sense of good taste. Two parlours divided by a door once comprised the living area on the east side of the centre hall. The mantel in the front parlour is of walnut, incised and embellished with fine dentils. The rich, warm wood enhances a

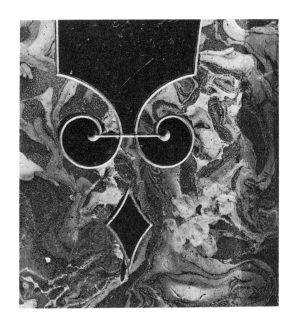

stone surround. The Library and Dining Room had almost identical mantelpieces. Unfortunately, the one in the Dining Room has at one time been treated to a coat of paint, but the Library mantelpiece, in the room now used as a kitchen, remains in splendid condition. Marble mantels were not uncommon in fine houses during this period, but the slate mantelpiece in the Wass House is an excellent example of *trompe-l'oeil* as it has been masterfully coloured to resemble marble. Marbelized slate mantels date from the middle of the nineteenth century in the United States, but the process did not attain broad acceptance until the last quarter of the century. Slate cost only two-thirds the price of marble and was much stronger, hence there was less likelihood of damage during shipment. After its arrival from the quarry, the slate was cut and chiseled for the desired ornamentation and carving before it was subjected to what was supposedly a secret process. After first being rubbed with pumice and polished with felt, the base colour was painted on. The slate was then dipped into a vat of water. Oil colours sprinkled on the surface of the water were manipulated with a brush and fanned to create a variegated appearance. The finish was then baked and polished and a coat of varnish applied to the mantel as a final step. Imitations of various kinds of marble were created by the introduction of appropriate colours. Gold tracery and an unusual tin hearth complete this fine example of craftsmanship in the William Wass House.

William Wass died in 1892, and two years later his wife and daughter presented a new

pipe organ at St. John's Church in his memory. Mary Wass died in 1903, and their daughter Rebecca remained in the house until her death in 1925. Like her father, she had been an active member of the Church, organizing the "Ever-Faithful Bible Class" in 1911, and later becoming the first woman trustee of the church.

W. S. Davis purchased the property in 1926 as an investment and rented the house to Courtland Freer, a retired bank manager and his wife. Freer, naming the house "Balsam Lawn" after the many trees Wass had planted, took great pride in the landscaping of the grounds. He maintained a dahlia farm on the property and gained considerable recognition within horticultural circles as well as among the citizenry of Oakville for whom he named many varieties. In 1951 T. A. McGillivray and his family moved to Oakville and into the Wass house, and it remained with that family for almost twenty-five years.

The showy cornices with bracket pairs and drop pendants and the magnificent hooded doorway supported by enormous scrolled brackets demonstrate that William Wass knew just what he wanted and that William Lee was well qualified to oblige him. The Wass House is a fine example of the joiner's skills at a time when mass production and mechanical decoration were becoming popular. At the same time, the building delicately balances a healthy degree of ostentatious bravado with an air of gentle dignity, for William Wass was both an Auctioneer and Churchman.

Circa 1883
St. Jude's Church

160 WILLIAM STREET

Oakville's first-recorded Anglican service was a celebration of the Eucharist by an itinerant clergyman in 1839. The Reverend Dr. Thomas Greene served the community in those first years, taking turns and sharing space with other Protestant denominations in a log school house on the banks of the Sixteen. The Methodists had a splendid three-hundred-seat structure of Neo-Classic design, but after just two years found themselves with a great financial burden and sold the building to the members of the Church of England. After considerable alterations, the building then standing on Lakeshore Road at the northwest corner of Thomas Street was dedicated as the Church of St. Jude.

In the same year, 1842, the Reverend George Warr arrived in Oakville to serve as the first incumbent of the new parish. St. Jude's then went under the charge of a number of rectors until 1851 when the Reverend Robert Shanklin took over the congregation. Described as a man of great literacy and musical tastes, he was instrumental in establishing a four-piece orchestra in the gallery and introducing a harmonium in the service. It was during Shanklin's term that a plot of ground was purchased a mile west of the town for a cemetery and as a site of a large, square brick parsonage later to be known as "Holyrood." The parsonage was sold many years afterwards, as its distant location from the church and proximity to the lake caused an unfortunate incident when a clergyman, lost in a blizzard, was only saved from a cruel death by his faithful dog.

In 1869 the Reverend J. B. Worrell took over the thriving parish, and within ten years it became evident that the congregation had outgrown the existing church and plans were begun to finance the erection of a new building at the corner of Thomas and William Streets. On April 23, 1883, workmen began to dig the foundation, and on the thirteenth of June 1883 the cornerstone was laid by the Most Worshipful Daniel Spry. The new church was officially opened on Sunday, December 16, 1883, by the Reverend Mr. Mockridge. George Sumner, who lived across the street, wrote in his diary that the first wedding to take place in the new English Church was between Herbert Litchfield and Miss Armstrong on Wednesday, March 19, 1884.

Many improvements and additions were made over the ensuing years, and in 1887 the Sunday School with its beautiful window commemorating Queen Victoria's Jubilee was completed. The window was a gift of Mr. Christopher Armstrong, a long-time warden. The year 1893 saw the introduction of electric lighting in St. Jude's. However, the steam plant that generated the power, situated in the "Worn Doorstep" on the shore of the lake between Dunn and George Streets, was far from dependable, and oil lamps served as auxiliary lighting for many years. The tower was completed in 1896 and at the time boasted an iron pinnacle on each of its topmost corners. In 1930 a severe storm toppled one of the pinnacles, and the remaining three were wisely taken down. The tower also boasted one of the best views of the surrounding countryside, and for five cents and a good climb the town was yours to behold.

In 1890 the income of St. Jude's Church consisted of $477 from collection plate offerings and $529 as pew rental. The total income was $1,006. This was not a great sum but expenses were not excessive either. The expenditures — the rector's stipend of $600, the fee for blowing the organ by hand pump $16, coal $58, cutting wood 50c, wine $4.90, and taxes $7.28 — totalled $686.68.

In 1903, after thirty-five years of dedicated service, the man who guided the building and growth of the new St. Jude's Church, the Reverend Canon J. B. Worrell, resigned his charge.

In 1913, just a week before Christmas, an overheated furnace ignited the floor of the nave, and only by the valiant efforts of the volunteer fire brigade was the building saved from total destruction. That year, Christmas Communion was gratefully celebrated in the Sunday School which was undergoing renovations at the time. In 1925, the Sunday School was further enlarged and a Parish Hall was erected. In 1927, W. S. Davis, a warden for fifty-one years, gave the Church two lots adjoining the church property; the Sexton's cottage and lot had already been donated by Mr. Davis. Earlier he had outfitted the nave with new oak pews. The generosity of this gentleman enabled the later planners to enlarge the church in 1956 to accommodate 450 members. These additions involved the extension of the main body of the structure to include a Narthex with a gallery over it, a larger Parish Hall, a Choir vestry and church offices.

The numerous additions over the years have not only been compatible with the original Gothic structure but have expanded it in character as well as size. The red brick interior walls of the nave and chancel, the fine display of stained glass, and the carved ceiling trusses are most impressive. Discreet polychromatic brickwork around the pointed arch openings of doorways and windows relieves the sobriety and creates a friendly mood. The exterior similarly exhibits skillful brickwork and pleasing design in the angle buttresses supporting the tower and crenellated parapet wall surrounding the top.

A. H. Lightbourn wrote in 1957, concluding a history of St. Jude's, that the church was indeed "a far cry from the log building on the banks of the Sixteen."

113

1883
The Odd Fellows and Masonic Halls

128-130 LAKESHORE ROAD EAST

The corner of Navy Street and Lakeshore Road was the hub of the mercantile trade in early Oakville. The southeast corner was an obvious choice when W. F. Romain decided in 1855 to put up a building. During the 1850s many brick buildings replaced the weather-board shops erected during the thirties, and Romain was not to be outdone by the iron-fronted Gage and Hagaman building. The Romain Block, or Navy Block, as it was sometimes called, was built of red brick carried over from Oswego. It stood three storeys high and covered a third the length of the block between Navy and Thomas Streets.

John Barclay, a purveyor of dry goods, groceries, and clothing, occupied the most westerly shop, and Peter MacDougald, a produce dealer, occupied the adjoining shop on the street level. Barclay lived over his place of business for a time on the second floor of the Romain Block. The White Oak Lodge No. 168, Ancient, Free, and Accepted Masons, formed in 1868, originally met in Robertson's Hardware Store, and later held their meetings on the third floor over Barclay's shop. The Orangemen, who had formed a lodge in Oakville in the early 1850s, moved their meetings from Paddy Smithwick's tavern to space over MacDougald's store. On a Sunday evening in the spring of 1883, the Negro bellboy at the Oakville House noticed smoke pouring out of the offices on the east end of the Romain Block. The alarm was sounded and a considerable quantity of stock was saved before the fire spread down to the lower floors. But by early morning almost the entire block from Navy to Thomas Street lay in ruin.

In the same year John Barclay moved into new quarters on the site of his previous shop.

The new two-storey building covered the westerly half of the old Romain Block site.

The Masons, who formed a new lodge in 1883, The Oakville Lodge No. 400 G.R.C., after surrendering the original charter because of political tensions in 1882, again occupied the space over the Barclay store. In 1923 they moved to their own building at Thomas and Church Streets. The Odd Fellows had met in a hall in the easterly end of the Romain Block and after the fire they purchased the easterly half of the new building. The Odd Fellows let out the shop below to the local newspaper. George King, son of William McKenzie King, had operated the *Standard* for several years, but with the loss of the presses in the fire he departed Oakville to live in the West. For a time the local paper was known as the *Express*, but later in 1883 it changed its name again. The *Star*, as it was then known, occupied the lower floor for many years. In 1887, just four years after the fire, a young lad of seventeen named Arthur Forster joined the paper as a printer. Within two years Forster bought the business and continued as editor and publisher for forty years. The editorial policy was proclaimed as "independent in politics, devoted to local interests and indefatigable advocate of good roads."

The Independent Order of Odd Fellows instituted Lodge No. 132 in Oakville in 1874. They became incorporated in 1878 and celebrated the occasion with a ball that was held in the Town Hall and attended by thirty-six couples. At one time the membership of this charitable fraternity swelled to over one hundred, but over the years their numbers have dwindled to the size when the group first incorporated.

Today the Odd Fellows enter by the same

stout, six-panel door off the street as early members did. The long, high-ceilinged passageway with its deeply moulded baseboards has not changed. A flight of six steps, a landing, and then twelve more steps lead to another six-panel door, surmounted by a transom light. Through the opened door the spacious meeting room is revealed. The shoulder-high wainscoting has been replaced by a lower, less dramatic covering in later years. Gone are the two wood stoves that once heated the quarters, and gone from the lodge hall floor is the large carpet, embellished with the chain-link symbol of the fraternity.

The two halves of the building were each originally capped with a pediment bearing a date stone. The westerly half once occupied by the Masons is now blank but for the year. The Odd Fellows inscription remains, as does the symbolic three-link chain representing friendship, love, and truth. The block is a relatively simple common bond brick structure but the incised pattern on the stone lintels and the arched brick details add texture and interest. A feeling of exuberance prevails about the structure, and this can be attributed to the heavy-handed wood trim. Although many have disappeared, the remaining wooden urns perched on the uppermost reaches present a fanciful image. Massive brackets and pairs of lesser brackets support a heavy, deeply moulded cornice. The pair of doors in the centre of the structure are crowned by another pediment resplendent with a sunburst design and topped with yet another wooden urn. Heavy pilasters and an even more massive cornice frame the ever-changing, twentieth-century store fronts, but the Odd Fellow Hall lives on.

1883
ODD FELLOWS HALL

1883

Circa 1884
The William Busby Store

191-195 LAKESHORE ROAD EAST

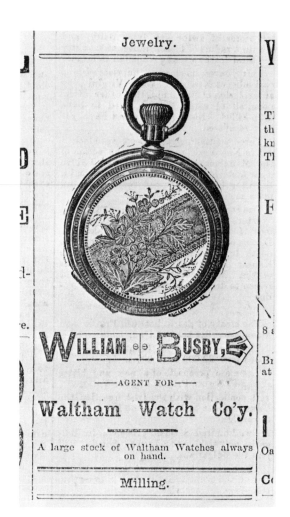

As a young lad of eleven years, William Busby journeyed with his parents and family from Ashley, Northamptonshire, England, to set sail for Canada. They departed late in the year 1862. Disease swept through the passengers of the vessel, and William's mother died on January 1, 1863, soon after their arrival in Oakville. A sister, Clara, died in July, and two years later his young brother George died, leaving William and three sisters. In 1867 William's father, George Busby, married Elizabeth Gibbons Walker, a widow with five children, and four more children were born to them. In *Lovell's Directory* of 1871, George Busby is listed as a teamster, or carter. George served as a Private in the 1st Oakville Rifle Company, and he and his wife were original members of the Salvation Army in Oakville. George and Elizabeth Busby both died in the typhoid epidemic of 1889.

When he was not in school, young William hired out at age thirteen to a local farmer. Shortly thereafter he became apprenticed to Aaron Matthews, an artist and repairer of clocks and watches who was responsible for tending the clocks at the Town Hall and the School House. William Busby learned the trade well, and after a stint in Hamilton he returned to Oakville and started in business for himself in 1881.

Many years earlier, in 1831, William Uptegrave purchased the lot on the southeast corner of George Street and Lakeshore Road and had a tavern erected. A few years later, Uptegrave leased the Royal Exchange, as it was called, and moved across the street to set up another tavern to the west of Charles Davis the shoemaker. John A. Williams reminisced in his daily journal around 1900 that "Old Mr. Uptegrave kept tavern in house where W. S. Davis office now stands." The Land Title records show that in 1884 William Busby purchased the westerly part of lot F in block 6 for $800. This portion of the lot was

where William Uptegrave had built his second tavern. William Busby's daughter, Miss Mary Busby, recalls that her father joined two old buildings together before greatly "modernizing the exterior."

During renovations in 1933, confirmation of an early dating of the structure was made with the discovery of old wallpaper applied directly to wide planks in the hall of the original entry, and pinned and mortised, hand-adzed and half-round timbers are still evident in the cellar today. No doubt William Busby took Uptegrave's tavern and another old building and had them drawn up in a line to create a long narrow structure, forming 191-195 Lakeshore Road East. A coat of smooth stucco was applied over the weatherboard siding, and the finish was then scored to imitate courses of ashlar block. Pairs of gracefully swooping brackets decorated with large drops were fitted under the projecting gable in an attempt to impart some of the splendour of the current Victorian taste.

William married Mary Jane Walker and they had four children; Allen, Irene, George, and Mary. The family lived over the shop, entering by a pair of doors on the westerly corner of the building. These doors have since been moved, as has the stairway, to an addition on the west side. A parlour ran the breadth of the building across the front of the second storey, and bedrooms were located at the rear. On the street level, at the back of the shop, a door led to a large dining room, and further back a kitchen. Although it no longer exists, a large bay projected from the dining room and the room above, offering a fine view of the side yard which was resplendent with gardens and a gazebo.

In the booklet *Picturesque Oakville* published in 1904, the following notation appeared:

"The jewellery line, too, is well represented by W. Busby, who has been in business since

1881, and a resident since 1862. Besides a very fine assortment of jewellery, watches, etc., Mr. Busby keeps a full supply of stationery, and has a unique display of cut glass and fine china. In these various branches, always well-stocked, a considerable trade is done every year, especially in watch adjusting, which is a feature of the business; only the best skill is employed. Here also is the central office of the Bell Telephone Company, of whom Mr. Busby is local manager. Along with his other duties Mr. Busby acts as agent for the Western Fire Insurance Company."

Right up until 1933, the year he died, William Busby with his white beard could be seen in the window of his shop, sitting at a bench or treadle lathe, repairing watches, clocks, and jewellery. His death ended forty years of service as a member of the Board of Education and forty-five years as a Member of Board of Trustees of St. John's Church. William Busby's daughters continued to operate the shop for a number of years and finally sold it after ninety-five years of family ownership.

Circa 1887
The Anderson Block

132-134 LAKESHORE ROAD EAST

The Anderson Block stands on land that was once covered by the easterly portion of the Romain Block. Before it was destroyed in the fire of 1883, the Romain Block housed many of the town's most important mercantile operations. James Bell Forsyth Chisholm, a druggist and soap factor, occupied a store which was taken over by druggist C. W. Pearce in the late 1860s. Here also, Moses McCraney, a general merchant who had earlier operated a store in Bronte, and J. G. Heiter, a grocer, maintained shops. William and Andrew Robertson operated a hardware store on the premises, and for a while Dr. E. J. Ogden kept an office there. The upper storey was the location of a public hall, and it was there, in Lewis Hall, that William Wass conducted his auctions of "town lots, cleared farms and wild lands, mercantile goods." The Odd Fellow's Hall and the *Standard* newspaper office shared the second floor, and it was in the newspaper office at the east end of the block, over McCraney's store, that the great conflagration started.

The Romain Block was in ashes, but they were hardly cool when building had commenced on the westerly portion of the land. The easterly half was to lie vacant for four years before Cyrus W. Anderson chose to establish a new bank on the site. There he had a two-storey structure erected abutting the new home of the Odd Fellows and the Masons. The easterly portion of the Anderson Block, as it was known, was let to the Morden Fuel Company and Ashton's Drug Store. The upper storey again provided the town with a hall for the general public, and George Sumner wrote of numerous parties and dances "up in Anderson's hall" during the 1890s.

Anderson took up the westerly half of the lower floor, and here he and his sons oper-

ated one of their two banks, the other being in Palmerston. Anderson and his wife Margaret had nine children, and of their six sons Egbert appears to have been most involved with Anderson's Bank in Oakville. In his diary, Sumner, then the town constable, described the sensational hold-up on April 27, 1897. "Quite a commotion in town. Anderson's Bank blown open and $750.00 taken. S. S. Craig's Horse and Rig stolen. Bert Anderson and I went to Toronto. Saw Detective Murray of the Gov. department." He wrote again on Thursday, December 18, 1902: "Another sensation today, the firm of C. W. Anderson & Sons Bankers went into liquidation. Liabilities supposed to be $100,000 or over. Many have lost their all. Our loss $65.00." More than $200,000 was involved in the failure of Anderson's Bank, and approximately 500 depositors collected 2½-cents on the dollar. The Town of Oakville lost its newly collected tax money, and Knox Church lost its hard-earned collection money.

Anderson and his sons lost many possessions, as Sumner noted in January. "They seized Bert Anderson's things when they were loaded up for Toronto." The Anderson assets included a farm east of Allan Street with a large home that stood where apartments now stand, as well as the Anderson Block. The Bank of Hamilton took over these assets, and it was W. S. Davis, manager of the bank, who subdivided the Anderson Farm into the Brantwood Survey.

Cyrus W. Anderson died at age eighty-two in October of 1920 and his obituary read:

"Born in Oakville on the old homestead. Son of Jos. Brant Anderson who was named after the Indian chief, Joseph Brant. From his father, Cyrus inherited the farm on the 7th line, Trafalgar, and the farm in town, now

known as Brantwood Survey. He built the large house known as "Grit Anchorage." All leading Liberals were entertained there and Mr. Anderson made a practice of placing a lamp in every window of the large house on every occasion when a Liberal was elected in Halton."

Today the Anderson Block is a town-owned property, and during the 1950s it served as the Town Clerk's Office and Police Station. Anderson's Hall on the upper storey provided a meeting place for the Town Council during those years.

This red brick, common bond edifice has had many tenants since Anderson's day, and like most nineteenth-century commercial blocks only the exterior of the second storey retains the original character. The façade is divided by six blind arcades, each bearing a keystone and containing a single window headed with a lesser keystone. Decorative panels of brickwork and a stepped parapet wall add textural interest to the second storey. The first-floor interior has been divided by partitions and covered with panelling while the second-floor interior, like the exterior, has undergone fewer changes. Here deeply moulded doorcases are still crowned by transom lights, while turn-of-the-century, tongue-and-groove wainscoting and a picture rail still cling to the walls of Anderson's Hall.

The Anderson Block is surely not as resplendent as its neighbour to the west, and it would invariably go unnoticed unless one happens to look above the street-level façades. In fact there are two distinctly different streetscapes—the lower level, representing the constantly changing twentieth century; and the upper, the original of the nineteenth century.

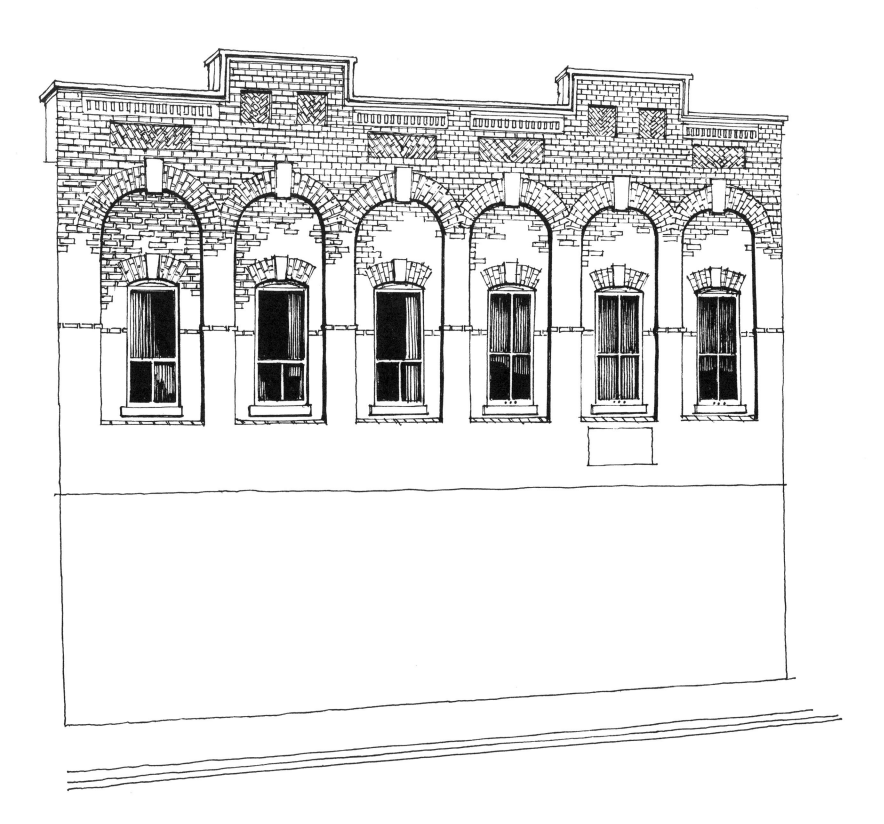

Circa 1887
The James Freestone House

207 REYNOLDS STREET

James Freestone was one of seven children of Mary and John Freestone, who was a plasterer from Ashley, Northamptonshire, England. As their eldest son, James remained a bachelor for many years, and setting an example for his younger brother John he put aside his earnings as a bricklayer in order to buy land. In 1877 James Freestone purchased the corner lot at Reynolds Street and Palmer Avenue, comprising two separate parcels of land, from R. K. Chisholm for the sum of $240. A year later he purchased another parcel adjoining this property on the northern boundary.

To further his career as a bricklayer, James moved to Toronto about 1885. There he lived in a hotel on Front Street until he married Emily Ann Wake of Oakville. The couple then took up residence in Toronto where James was busily employed. He built their first home in the Spadina-Queen area and was responsible for erecting many fine dwellings in the Casa Loma district. Acting as both a bricklayer and a foreman, James Freestone applied his skills to the fancy brickwork arches and ornate door surrounds on many commercial buildings as well.

In 1887 James sold the northerly half of the parcel adjoining his corner lot on Reynolds Street to his brother George. George Freestone was a plasterer like his father, and it is probable that both houses—the James Freestone House on the corner and the George Freestone House north of it—were built in that year. The Collector's Rolls of the following year, 1888, report that both properties had tenants and that each lot was assessed at a value that indicated a substantial dwelling. Although George's house is finished in stucco, inscribed with ashlar block delineations, and James' is constructed of polychrome brickwork, each bears bargeboards of an identical fret-work pattern. In 1891 James sold the other half of the lot to George, giving him the present frontage of 213 Reynolds Street.

James' brother John lived in the Melancthon Simpson House, and later built a new house on his back lot at 236 Reynolds Street, while brother Robert lived at 153 Reynolds. It seemed only fitting in 1964 that the Town of Oakville changed Sheddon Avenue to Freestone Lane in honour of the family that contributed so much to the development of the neighbourhood.

In 1924 James Freestone and his wife Emily sold the house to Frederick "Mac" McCallum and his wife of one year. McCallum, who had come to town as a banker, worked as a wool broker and later secured a position as Customs Officer, and he remained in that position until transferred to Hamilton. McCallum continued to live in Oakville, and during his residency a white picket fence surrounded the house, the well, and the barn where McCallum, like many other residents, kept his chickens. Four children were born to the McCallums in the living room of the house, and it was only with the passing away of Mrs. McCallum that the house came into the possession of the third owner in July 1977.

The Freestone House originally exhibited three chimneys. Two chimneys which serviced the stoves were located on the south and east walls, and a fireplace opening was discovered on the north wall in the living room when the McCallums installed a fireplace in that location in 1945. The back verandah on the tail was enclosed at the same time.

This "L" shaped red brick house is very much in the style of the Ontario farmhouse, even though it shows no evidence of ever having the front verandah so typical of the classical examples of this building style. Although many of the features of the Victorian fashion are present, as evidenced in the decorative bargeboard, the buff-coloured brick quoins and arches, the segmental and round-headed windows, and the bracketed bay, the structure retains a disciplined, orderly appearance.

Circa 1888
Knox Presbyterian Church

89 DUNN STREET

The first Presbyterian service in Oakville was held in a small, log public hall in 1833. These first services were conducted by the Reverend Alexander Gale, a missionary sent out from Scotland, who travelled from charge to charge by horseback. Ceremonies and services were also held in Dr. Urquart's residence and in the shop of cabinetmaker David Duff.

From the original eleven members, the congregation grew in numbers and in financial stability, enabling them to commission, in 1849, the construction of a church of their own. James McDonald Sr. built, on William Street, a frame structure with large windows and a high pulpit in 1850, and it was that year that the congregation acquired a pastor of their own in the Reverend James Nisbet. The congregation numbered ninety-eight in 1866, and when the Reverend Mr. Meikle replaced Nisbet in 1867 further increases took place. Under the leadership of the Reverend Mr. Meikle, the roll grew from 147 in 1871 to 203 members in 1877.

During these years communion services began at 10:00 a.m. and continued until 2:00 p.m. Children were permitted to leave the service to eat lunch and return afterwards. Collection envelopes were introduced in 1881 but were strongly opposed by a conservative

element and were hastily withdrawn and replaced by pew rent. During the early 1880s the ranks of the congregation thinned somewhat to 149 in 1884, as many members swung over to the new Methodist Church. The erosion gradually halted, and by 1887 the 193 adherents of the Presbyterian Church, perhaps in an attempt to hold the flock together, expressed their wishes for a more pretentious place of worship. In 1887 they purchased the White Oak Hotel on Lakeshore Road at Dunn Street, cut it into three sections, moved off the sections, and began construction of their new church. James McDonald Jr., son of the carpenter who constructed the first Presbyterian Church, built the imposing new structure for a cost of $10,800. The total cost of the new building, according to George Sumner's diary, was almost $16,000, and it seems that McDonald accepted the old church building as partial payment. The cornerstone was laid by Agnes Marlatt, and on Sunday, May 23, 1888, the Reverend Dr. Cochrane conducted the opening service.

Until 1873 a "precentor" and the ring of a tuning fork led the singing of hymns in the Oakville Presbyterian Church, but in that year certain factions were successful in introducing a motion that would permit the use of

musical instruments. However, it was not until 1894, six years after the new church was opened, that conservative opposition allowed the installation of a pipe organ, and on February 25, 1906, the newly acquired steeple bell, cast in New York, rang in the tower for the first time.

In 1920 the interior was remodelled considerably, and a fine stained-glass window depicting the Last Supper, a tribute from C. G. Marlatt to the lads of the congregation who fell in the Great War, was placed in the newly created chancel. Several windows in the church were created by the Toronto firm of Robert McCausland Limited. At this time the choir seating was removed from its original position, straight across the front of the church and so was the organ which had been obscured behind the choir stalls. The main floor pews were replaced, but the original pews with beautifully decorative cast-iron ends still serve in the gallery. The face of the gallery is embellished with a decorative frieze of cast-iron panels containing a floral design. The exposed wood structure on the ceiling of the nave and the panels on the sides of the chancel display some very fine carving in the same spirit. Each side of the nave carries a small gable containing a dramatic pointed arch window. Moulded wooden mullions de-

123

fine the geometric tracery of the three lesser arches and the circular light within, just as the new window of the 1920s displays a form of flowing tracery typical of the medieval architecture, the basis of the design of the entire structure.

This Gothic style church, with its high, pointed arch windows and buttresses reinforcing the tower walls, presents a striking silhouette with an octagonal spire, corner pinnacles, and dormers. However, a variety of architectural influences and popular building materials of the time can be seen in the hooded labels of Tudor design over the window and door openings, the fish-scale shingles on the steeple, and the polychromatic brickwork of the Victorian era to add colour to the Gothic austerity.

Further additions, in character with the main structure, were added in 1956 and in 1965 to meet the needs of a growing congregation. The early congregation who built this fine Gothic building may seem overly conservative today. Consequently it comes as a surprise to discover that the nave is sloped with pronounced back-to-front pitch much like a theatre. Knox Presbyterian Church was well ahead of its time.

1888
The Cecil G. Marlatt House

43 DUNN STREET

Thompson Smith started a tannery in the mid-1850s, on the west bank of the Sixteen, just about the time that Cecil Gustavus Marlatt was born. The business was operated by Smith for many years, and after his death it continued to flourish under various managers, as the surrounding countryside produced greater numbers of cattle. In 1871 the tannery was valued at $20,559 and employed eighteen men. In the seventies Christopher Armstrong took over the operation, and a decade later it became known as Armstrong and Company when Stafford Marlatt and Captain Maurice Felan became principal stockholders. In the late 1880s Stafford Marlatt bought out Felan's interest in the tannery and installed his two sons, Wilbur and Cecil. A business directory of 1888-89 lists the firm of Marlatt and Armstrong as "mfgs. patent enamelled and carriage leathers & tanners." The tannery of Marlatt & Armstrong, as one of the largest employers in Oakville, was by far the most important industry in the town. The tannery grew in size as the years passed, and in addition to producing glove leathers and patent leathers for shoes, the leather that had been produced for carriages was used in the upholstery of automobile seats.

In 1888 Cecil G. Marlatt and his wife Agnes moved into their new home at the corner of Dunn and King Streets. However, tragedy struck in December of that year, when the twenty-six-year-old Agnes died leaving Marlatt with an infant son. Four years later Mar-latt married a distant relative, Sarah Stafford Marlatt. Cecil and "Birdie," as she was always known, raised a son and three daughters in the big house. Staunch Presbyterians, the family were members of Knox Presbyterian Church where Marlatt's first wife Agnes had laid the cornerstone the year she died. It was to Knox that "Birdie" presented a bell for the tower, and later C.G. donated a memorial window after the Great War. Marlatt served as both Councillor and Reeve and, coming from a strong Grit background, was President of the Oakville Liberals Club. He and his brother Wilbur and Armstrong, their business partner, were owners of the racing yacht *Aggie* that Captain Andrew had built. Skippered by Cecil Marlatt, who also served as Commodore of the Royal Canadian Yacht Club, the *Aggie* won countless trophies and held the Club championships for many years.

In 1898 Marlatt purchased the easterly two thirds of the block, enclosing the property by a high white wooden fence. Within the grounds were numerous out-buildings, including a green house, a tool house, a root cellar, and a playhouse for the Marlatt children, as well as two fish ponds. Afternoon tea was served in a large summerhouse overlooking a cricket pitch and a lawn tennis court. A vegetable garden was laid out on land Marlatt purchased on the south side of King Street, and there a stable sheltered a carriage, horses, and a cow. The stable later gave way to a garage for a new motor car.

The family kept a serving staff of four: a gardener, a chauffeur, and two inside help. Two barrels of fine wine arrived annually from France, a red and a white, which the staff decanted into bottles and racked in a cellar wine cupboard. Sumner recorded in 1895: "Mr. C.G. Marlatt's house was on fire this afternoon, Incendiary—done well to get out. Supposed to be a tramp, they are a great nuisance." Even after the episode tramps were never turned away, and a daughter, Mrs. Mary Oliver, recalls that when they appeared at the rear door they were always given something to eat. Just the same, a ladder was permanently positioned thereafter in the upper hall, beneath a trap-door leading to the roof, and two large pails filled with water were kept on a platform near the opening. The Marlatt home was the scene of large garden parties and many gatherings with great frivolity, but it all came crashing to an end when in the mid-1920s, without warning, the Tannery failed. With Oakville's largest industry gone, large numbers of men were thrown out of work, and the vast building complex went empty. The Marlatts lost their home that reportedly cost $8,000 to build and all but a few of their household furnishings.

After being occupied for a number of years by several families, in 1938 the bank sold the Marlatt house to Stanley Steele Russell. Russell, his wife, and five children lived on the second and third floors. His business, a funeral parlour, took up the ground floor. Vari-

ous alterations were made to the house as the business grew, and in 1953 S. S. Russell and his wife moved out of the house. His son William, who eventually was to run the business, his wife, and child took over the upstairs apartment. William Russell and his family remained in the house until 1960, when they moved to one of the houses that had been erected on the old Marlatt property, and the third storey quarters were given over to staff from the funeral parlour. In 1976 the business was closed and the old Marlatt House was sold to once again become a private dwelling.

Boldly turned spools and spindles demonstrating the woodworker's skills once decorated a softly curving verandah. The verandah sheltered a vestibule enclosed by two sets of double doors, each surmounted by an etched glass transom light. The entire porch and entry were replaced by the Russells who, during the course of renovations, discovered pencilled on an interior wall stud "This house was built in 1888." The inscription also bore the name of the carpenter which, unfortunately, has been lost. Two parlours on the north side were made one when the dividing wall and doorway were removed. In the parlours cast-iron radiator covers emblazoned with "1888" bear out the carpenter's message. The door openings off the hallway were reduced in height, modifying the door architrave and causing the loss of the corner

medallions. The corner medallions can still be found on the window architraves. The dining room is across the broad hall from the parlour, and here the Marlatts left a legacy in a leather wainscoting, finely tooled in a floral design. Beyond the dining room, there once was a butler's pantry with a passthrough to the kitchen. The pantry is gone, and so is the wood cookstove that stood in the kitchen. A staircase still rises steeply from the rear to the servants' quarters.

The main staircase rises from a large front entry hall. The bannister and spindles, now painted, were originally a dark walnut. The newel post at the foot of the stairs was once capped by a heavy brass electric lantern with coloured glass. The staircase climbs to a landing illuminated by a fine stained glass window which the Marlatt children called "The Apple Lady." The window bears the signature J. McCausland & Sons and the date "1888." Robert McCausland Ltd. of Toronto still retain the original "cartoon" for the Marlatt window in their files.

Originally there were four bedrooms on the second floor, each with a glass transom light over the door. Mrs. Mary Oliver remembers that the transoms were always kept closed to keep out the cigar smoke on the nights her father entertained the men's whist club. The room over the dining room was reserved for guests and offered a gold-trimmed porcelain

wash basin. The two bedrooms on the north side have been made into one commodious master bedroom and corresponds to the plan below. A fireplace with a hearth of glazed tiles set in a diamond pattern remains intact although the mantelpiece has been changed. Outside the bathroom there once was a silver-collared opening on the wall. When blown into, a whistle was activated, and the help was summoned down from their third-floor quarters or from the main floor. Young Kenneth Dean Marlatt shared the third floor, occupying the larger of the three rooms. From a small platform access could be gained to the tower room which provided him with a splendid view of the lake.

The dramatic tower, with steeply pitched roof and dormers, is set at a forty-five degree angle to the main block. Large bays project from both the westerly and southerly walls. Each bay is crowned by a heavy, protruding gable, decorated with ornate bargeboards and fish-scale shingles. The whole gives the appearance of being supported solely by the massive cornice and over-sized brackets. The common bond brickwork is relieved by a variety of brick pattern bands. A fanciful chimney rises up the wall of the southerly gable and pierces the roof in a most dramatic fashion. The Marlatt House typifies the picturesque style of Victorian architecture illustrated in the numerous pattern books available during the 1880s.

Circa 1893
The Charles Pettit Chisholm House

164 TRAFALGAR ROAD

In 1839 William Chisholm sold the land where this house now stands to his second-eldest son, John Alexander Chisholm. This was one of many pieces of land John purchased, and he was eventually responsible for the development of several surveys. John himself lived further north on Trafalgar Road on a large farm where he cleared the land and had a house built. It seems that a modest frame building was erected on the site of the present house at 164 Trafalgar Road, for in 1866 the Collector's Rolls lists the Reverend R. Scott as tenant, and in 1873 Albert Hilliard is listed as a tenant or householder, in a dwelling owned by John A. Chisholm.

John and his wife Sarah, whom he married in 1843, had four sons, and three of them became involved in various business ventures on the Chisholm farm. During the sixties, with the phenomenal success of the Oakville strawberry industry, John, perhaps inspired by his neighbour John Cross, began manufacturing berry boxes in a shed on his farm. In 1871 the business employed four men and eight boys and was capable of turning out 300,000 baskets during the winter months. John's son, Charles, was what in those days people described as a "mechanic." Intrigued by machinery, his inventive mind was responsible for the development of a paring machine that shaved from logs slivers of wood thin enough for fruit baskets. John A. Chisholm Sr. died in 1874, but two of his

sons, Charles and William, continued the enterprise and purchased the empty Victoria Brewery across Trafalgar Road, converting it into a highly productive basket factory. An advertisement in the *Great Western Railway Directory* of 1845-75 states: "W. B. & C.P. Chisholm, manufacturers of Berry Boxes, Plant Boxes, Grease Boxes, Lard Caddies, and every description of Veneer-cut Box material—Oakville, Ont."

In 1877 the partnership was dissolved, with William continuing the business on his own. Charles and his brother John Alexander conducted numerous experiments to develop a method of processing vegetables by evaporation and pursued their idea. Together they developed an operation whereby vegetables and fruits were evaporated, packaged, and sold throughout the world.

In 1881 Charles married the twenty-four-year-old Christina Kate Chisholm at the home of her father Captain George Brock Chisholm. The couple had no children and possibly lived at the family home with his mother, Sarah. The business directory of 1884-85 records "Chas. P. Chisholm Canada Soup Co. Evaporated fruits & vegetables," but later in the eighties the Chisholm brothers made their biggest coup when an opportunity arose to market their discoveries in the United States. By far their most significant invention was a machine that could shell peas, and Robert Scott, an inventor from Ohio, intrigued by the potential

for the machine below the border, suggested improvements and entered into partnership with the Chisholms. The resulting relationship was most successful, and the factory in New York State flourished. In 1886, Charles and his wife Christina, his brother John, and their mother Sarah took out a mortgage against the lot in block 89 where the house now stands as well as on other family lands for the sum of $4,050. This money may well have been utilized to finance this business venture.

In 1890 Charles is recorded as a tenant at 164 Trafalgar Road and his mother as owner. In 1891 Sarah sold the lot to her son Charles for $1,500. At forty-five, Charles, by then a most successful businessman, was in a position to have a new residence built for himself and his wife of ten years. Between 1890 and 1894 the assessment on the property increased almost three hundred percent, indicating Chisholm had the existing frame house either moved and replaced or enclosed with brick and increased in size. Charles died in 1914 at age sixty-eight, but his widow Christina lived there until about 1923, and two years before her death in 1942 she granted the property to Esther Anna Chisholm, a young widow with three children. The house remained in the Chisholm family for over seventy years.

The Chisholm House forms an "L" shape with a gable end facing the street. Originally a verandah bordered the house on two sides,

with rows of spool-work and a series of fret-work bracketed columns that served to disguise the unbalanced window arrangement of the front facade. Once crowned with king-posts, the gable ends, faced with decorative wooden shingles, still exhibit enormous bargeboards composed of a complex geometric design that includes fans, quatrefoils, and sunburst patterns. The ballroom that extends northward from the rear of the structure was added shortly after the house was built and was the scene of many parties and large family gatherings, even after Charles passed away. The interior of the ballroom received the benefit of additional illumination when the present curved roof replaced a conventional roof permitting sunlight to filter through translucent panels set between the ceiling beams. A massive brick fireplace displaying three recessed niches is set in a bay on the westerly wall, while the orchestra at one time performed from a raised platform in a bay that projects from the north end of the ballroom. At the turn of the century, Austrian blinds graced the windows, paintings suspended on wires from a picture rail adorned the walls, and a *portière* hung in the archway leading to the main part of the house. The Charles Pettit Chisholm House is one of the last great houses built in the nineteenth century in old Oakville. Stripped of many of the frivolous details typical of the era, it has survived only by submitting to division into apartments. One has to believe that if the grand verandah complete with spools, spindles, and fretwork patterns were again to embellish this late-Victorian house, it would be even more impressive today than when it was built.

This selection of forty-five buildings is representative of old Oakville's architectural heritage, but these structures are only a fraction of the total number of nineteenth-century buildings still standing. Many have been altered beyond recognition, while others had little to distinguish them when they were first erected. Nonetheless, beneath layers of asbestos and aluminum, many more have carefully kept hidden not only their history but also their future potential. It is our hope that this book will enable the readers to more readily identify these early structures, and that with additional research the personalities of these buildings and their builders will be revealed.

THE ARTISANS

The men who determined the physical
appearance of Oakville were, in general, the
men who commissioned the buildings, but it
was the craftsmen who physically gave the
town its shape. The following compilation
records, by decade, from the time of the great
building boom, the name and trade of those
artisans listed in the archival records
available to the authors. The trades are
designated by the following abbreviations:

Architect	ARCH
Bricklayer	BR
Brickmaker	BM
Builder	BU
Carpenter	CA
Contractor	CO
Gilder	GI
Glazier	GL
Grainer	GR
Joiner	JO
Mason	MA
Master Builder	MASBU
Mill Operator	MO
Painter	PA
Paper Hanger	PH
Plasterer	PL
Whitewasher	WW

1850s

Best, Thos.	PL
Boon, Isaac	MA
Boon, Joseph	BR
Calvin, James	PA, GL
Calvin, Thomas	PA, GL
Campbell, Duncan	CA
Coughlan, Thomas	ARCH
Cowton, John	PA
Cronkrite, Hiram	CA
Cronkrite, William	CA
Cross, John	CA
Durant, Edward	BR
Frampton, John	PA
Gallie, John	BU
Hall, John	BU
Harcus, Thomas	CA
Heatley, John	BR
Henry, William	MA
Home, John	MA
Jones, W. H.	PA, GL, PH
Jull, Samuel Sr.	BU
Leach, Robert	BU, CO
Lee, James	MO
Livingston, James	BU, ARCH
Londra, Dennis	CA
McCrum, Andrew	MA
McDermott, Thomas	CA
McDonald, James	CA, BU
McElroy, John	BU
McLean, John	BU
Moulds, Wm.	BU, CO
Murray, John	BU
Nelson, Thomas	MA
Nisbet, Thomas	JO
Patterson, David	CA, BU
Potter, John	JO
Rogers, George	PA
Snell, Charles	CO, BU
Thompson, James	CA
Wickfire, Orlow	MASBU
Young, John	CA

1860s

Boon, Isaac	PL
Boon, Joseph	MA
Brady, John	CA
Butler, John	CA
Campbell, Justus	CA
Clark, Isaac	CA
Connor, James	CA
Coote, George	CA
Coote, William	CA
Doty, Pharis	MO
Duncan, Benedict	WW
Frampton, John Sr.	PA, GI
Frampton, John Jr.	PL, GI
Freestone, John	PL
Hall, James	PL
Husband, George	PL
Jackson, Robert	CA, BU
Jones, W. H.	PA
Jull, Samuel Sr.	CA
Jull, Samuel Jr.	CA
Karkruff, Samuel	CA
Kenney, M.	PA
Lebarr, Andrew	CA
Lebarr, James	CA
Lee, Wm.	BU, MO
McDonald, James Sr.	CA, BU
McDonald, James Jr.	CA, BU
Mapes, Alfred	CA
Moulds, Wm.	CA
Ogden, E. J.	MO
Patterson, David	CA, JO
Rodney, James	CA
Shanks, John	CA
Slaney, Jeremiah	CA
Sumner, George	CA
Tetherington, Thomas	CA
Thompson, James	CA
Travis, P.	PL

1870s

Alton, D. W.	CA
Baird, John	PA
Barton, Charles	WW
Beals, John	CA
Boon, Isaac	MA
Boon, Joseph	MA, BR
Butler, John	CA
Buzzard, Jas.	PA
Caldwell, W. M.	PA, GL, PH
Calvin, James	PA, GL, GI
Calvin, Thomas	PA, GL, GI
Campbell, Donald	CA
Carson, C. D.	CA
Carson, G. R.	CA
Carson, Wm.	CA
Cavan, John	CA
Connor, James Sr.	BU
Connor, James Jr.	CA
Coote, Alexander	CA
Cronkrite, Thomas	CA
Cronkrite, William	CA
Dent, M. B.	CA
Doherty, John	CA
Duncan, Benedict	WW
Flewelling, John	CA
Forester, Wm.	PA
Frampton, John	PA
Freestone, John	PL, MA
Galbraith, George	CA
Galel, John	CA
Gallie, John	CA
Gallie, William	CA
Griffin, Kelly	CA
Hall, James	PA
Heatley, John	PA
Herbert, Herbert	PA
Hilliard, John	CA
Howell, Wesley	PA
Husband, George	PA
Jackson, Robert	CA
Karkruff, Samuel	CA
Leach, Chas.	CA
Leach, Wm.	CA
Lean, Ed.	PA
Lean, Wm. R.	PA
Lebarr, James	CA

1870s

Lebarr, H. M.	CA
Lee, Wm.	BU, MO
Litchfield, Herbert	CA
Long, Horatio Nelson	CA
Mapes, Alfred	CA
McCraney, Wm.	MO
McDonald, James Jr.	CA
McDonald, James Sr.	CA
McGraw, Wm.	CA
Milner, Jacob	CA
Nichols, Thos.	CA
Park, Joseph	CA
Patterson, David	CA
Patterson, Sam	CA
Pepper, Thomas	CA
Potter, John	CA
Rigney, F.	MA
Rourke, John	PA, GL, GR
Shewell, J. T.	BM
Spencer, John	BM
Sumner, George	CA
Tetherington, Thos.	CA
Ward, Wm.	WW
Wass, Wm.	MA
Webb, Thos.	PA
White, David	CA
White, Samuel	CA
Wood, R. S.	MO
Young, John	CA

1880s

Andrews, John	CA
Baines, Ed & Co.	PA MFTR.
Boon, Isaac	PA
Boon, Joseph	MA
Carson, W. T.	CA, BU, CO, MO
Chisholm, Charles	BM
Duncan, Benedict	WW
Doty, Pharis	MO
Gallie, John	CA
Heatley, John	PL
Herbert, Herbert	PA
Karkruff, Samuel	CA
King, James	PA
Leach, John	CA
Leach, Ransom	CA
Leach, Robert	CA
Lebarr, Henry	CA
McDonald, James Jr.	CA, MO
McDonald, Wm.	CA
McKinder, J.	CA, CO
Milner, Jacob	CA
Rourke, John	PA, GR
Tetherington, Thos.	CA
Woodell, John	CA

1890s

Andrew, Jas.	CA
Andrew, Thos.	CA
Bond, Wm.	MA
Boon, Joseph	MA
Brady, R. K.	CA
Brown, Henry	CA
Carson, W. T.	MO
Connor, Jas. Sr.	CA
Connor, Wm.	CA
Cronkrite, Wm.	CA
Doty, Chas.	MO
Duncan, Benedict	WW
Florio, Henry	MA
Forrester, James	PH
Forrester, Wm.	PA
Freestone, John	PL
Fulton, James	PA
Gallie, John	CA
Heatley, Wm.	PL
Karkruff, Wm.	CA
Leach, Wm.	CA
Mapes, Alfred	CA
McDonald, James Jr.	CA, BU
McKinder, Joel	CA
McKnight, John	CA
McPherson, Daniel	PA
Ribble, Chas.	CA
Ribble, Wm.	MA
Rourke, John	PA
Walsh, John	CA
Walsh, Thomas	CA
Wass, Wm.	PA, PH

INDEX OF BUILDINGS

GLOSSARY

Acanthus leaves: the scalloped leaves of a Mediterranean plant, often used as a design element for classical carved ornamentation.

Architrave: the lowest of three sections in a classical entablature, but more commonly the moulded frame surrounding a door or window opening.

Ashlar: the squared blocks of stonework used in courses.

Baluster: a rectangular or turned upright in a series, supporting a rail and forming a balustrade.

Balustrade: a row of balusters topped by a rail.

Bargeboard: a board placed against the incline of a gable and hiding the ends of the rafters or roof timbers.

Bay: external divisions of a building, window or door openings.

Bead: a small convex moulding.

Belvedere: a small look-out tower on the roof of a house.

Blind arcade: a series of arches applied to a solid wall.

Bracket: a curved or angular supporting piece, often scrolled, to carry a projecting weight.

Casement window: a window sash hung vertically, opening outwards or inwards on side hinges.

Chamfer: the surface created when a sharp edge or corner is bevelled.

Cornice: the top projecting section in a classical entablature; a moulding at the edge of a roof or a moulding at the angle where the ceiling meets the wall.

Course: a horizontal row of bricks or stones.

Dentil: a small, rectangular block used in a series as ornamentation below a cornice.

Drip course: a wall projection of brick or stone to throw off rain and protect an opening or joint beneath.

Dormer window: a window projecting from a sloping roof and with a roof of its own.

English bond: bricks laid in alternate courses of headers (ends) and stretchers (sides).

Façade: the face or front elevation of a building.

Fanlight: a fan-shaped window.

Fenestration: the arrangement of window openings.

Fret: cut-out ornamentation, usually in a geometric pattern.

Frieze: that part of a classical entablature between architrave and cornice; the band along the upper part of a wall immediately below the cornice.

Glazing bar: a narrow strip of wood that secures panes of glass in a door or window sash.

Keystone: the central tapered member of an arch.

Lantern: a projection with glazed sides on a roof; see Belvedere.

Lights: window panes.

Lintel: a horizontal member spanning an opening.

Medallion: a circular decorative panel.

Muntin: see Glazing bar.

Parapet: a low wall along the edge of a roof.

Pediment: a triangular section of a classical gable.

Pilaster: an upright, flat pillar which projects only slightly from a wall and simulates a column.

Quatrefoil: an ornamental medallion consisting of four arcs, and supported by cusps.

Quoins: projecting blocks at the corner of a building.

Return: a turn in moulding such as a cornice, usually at right angles from the front of a structure.

Sidelights: a vertical line of small glass panes on either side of a doorway.

Sill: the bottom member of a wall or window opening.

String course: a horizontal band, often projecting from the surface of a building.

Tail: an inferior appendage affixed to the rear of a structure, usually an addition to house a kitchen or summer kitchen.

Tenon: the end of a wooden timber cut to form a projection and fitting a corresponding hole or mortise in another timber.

Transom: a window over a door.

Wainscot: wood panelling on an interior wall, often below the chair rail.